God Thinks You're Positively Awesome

God Thinks You're Positively Awesome

**DISCOVER YOUR TRUE BEAUTY—
INSIDE AND OUT!**

Andrea Stephens

VINE BOOKS

SERVANT PUBLICATIONS
ANN ARBOR, MICHIGAN

Vine Books is an imprint of Servant Publications especially designed to serve evangelical Christians.

Scripture quotes were taken from the following versions of the Bible: TLB: The Living Bible, NASB: New American Standard Bible, NIV: New International Version, KJV: King James Version, NRSV: New Revised Standard Version. All rights reserved by the original copyright holders.

The publisher wishes to thank the following contributors to this book:

Brio magazine for permission to reprint several articles in this book. The original publication date appears after each article.

"Lisa Bevill: A Christie Brinkley Wannabe?" by Susie Shellenberger: © 1993, Focus on the Family. All rights reserved. International copyright secured. Used by permission.

"Pam Thum: Free to Be Herself!" by Susie Shellenberger. © 1994, Focus on the Family. All rights reserved. International copyright secured. Used by permission.

"Say G'Day to Rebecca St. James" by Susan Maffett. © 1995, Focus on the Family. All rights reserved. International copyright secured. Used by permission.

Campus Life magazine for permission to reprint "The Beautiful People," by Jim Long, which first appeared in the January 1992 edition of the magazine.

All the *Brio* readers and other teens who are quoted in this book. Thanks for your help!

Published by Servant Publications
P.O. Box 8617
Ann Arbor, Michigan 48107

Cover design: Left Coast Design, Portland, Oregon
Interior illustrations: Rosie Walker, pages 10, 24, 75, 76, 100, 102, 103, 104, 162

97 98 99 00 01 10 9 8 7 6 5 4 3 2

Printed in the United States of America
ISBN 0-89283-952-X

LIBRARY OF CONGRESS CATALOGING-IN-PUBLICATION DATA

Stepehens, Andrea.
God thinks you're positively awesome : discover your true beauty—inside and out! / Andrea Stephens.
    p. cm.
Summary: Encourages teenage girls to see themselves as unique creations of God, recognizing and rejecting superficial images of beauty, and offers practical advice on grooming, diet, and developing one's talents.
ISBN 1-56955-002-6
1. Teenage girls—Religous life.   2. Teenage girls—Conduct of life.   3. Beauty, Personal—Juvenile literature.   [1. Beauty, Personal.   2. Christian life.   3. Self-perception.]   I. Title.
BV4551.2.S73   1997
248.8'33—dc21   97-2109
                                                                                    CIP
                                                                                    AC

Table of Contents

Between Human Love and God's Love... Love Quiz: Find the Facts About God's Love!... *Girl Talk:* Nothing Can Separate You from God's Love!... *Girl Talk:* How Do *You* Show Your Love for God?... *Beauty Buster:* Stomping Out Self-Hate

Totally Awesome Truths About You!... The Way to True Beauty: A Christ-like Heart... *Girl Talk:* Share a Time When the Holy Spirit Gave You What You Needed *Right* When You Needed It... Uncover Your Power-Packed Potential!... *Up Close and Personal* with Heather Whitestone, Miss America 1995

Precious Gems of Inner Beauty... *Girl Talk:* What Is Inner Beauty?... The Beauty of a Gentle and Quiet Spirit... *Contentment Quiz:* Are You Gracious or Grumpcious?... A Joyful Person Is a Beautiful Person!... Teen Talk: Describe a Woman in Your Life Who Is Truly Beautiful... *Up Close and Personal* with 1997 *Brio* Girl Lindy Morgan... *Quiz:* Are You a Proverbs 31 Kind-a-Gal?... *Beauty Buster:* "Me! Me! Me!"... Random Acts of Kindness!... *Beauty Bonus:* Smart Shopping Tips!

God's Not Finished with You Yet!... Secrets to the Inner-Beauty Fast Track... *Up Close and Personal* with Contemporary Christian Artist Rebecca St. James... The Beautiful You Checklist... *Up Close and Personal* with Contemporary Christian Singer Pam Thum... Your Letter to the Lord

This book is dedicated to...

Elizabeth Wyans, my grandmother! Your gentle and loving way has always been a witness of your love for Christ and the beautiful heart you have because of him. May he wrap his everlasting arms of love around you even tighter during these twilight years. And thanks for letting me keep the little book, *Complete Sayings of Jesus,* that I swiped from your bookshelf when *I* was a teen! I promise to keep hiding his words in my heart.

Love ya!

And to...

Katie, Karlee, and Cassidy! I pray this book will help you battle the beauty message of a world that will be even wackier by the time you are teens! May you see that true beauty resides in the heart, especially when that heart belongs to Christ!

I love you up to the sky and back!
Aunt Annie

one

You Are "Babe" Material!
Discovering God's Beautiful Handiwork—You!

*Y*ep. That's "Babe." With a capital B! And it's YOU I'm talking about!

Your hair, wavy or straight; your eyes, round or slanted; your nose, wide or narrow; your lips, full or thin; your body, short or tall—You! Every single detail of your appearance joined together to give you "the LOOK"!

Oh, sure. Exactly what "look" is that?

I knew you were going to ask that question!

When you peer into that big bathroom mirror, the reflection you see staring back at you is God's perfect design! You have got "the look" that God custom-tailored just for you!

Yep. That's right. God himself. The same person who created the minuscule amoebas and the majestic mountains, the delicate purple orchid and the deep blue ocean, the sun that shines by day and the stars that glow by night.

The very same all-wise, all-knowing, all-powerful God, used his special touch to create YOU. Whew!

When he looks at you, he sees a young woman who is outrageously gorgeous, positively awesome! What do you see? Do you think of yourself as Babe material? Beautiful? Pretty? Awesome?

Attractive? Special? Well, God does! In his eyes you are a unique young woman with a beauty all her own.

Need some proof? No prob! Just follow me.

The Skillful Potter

There's a studio I want you to see. Pardon the creaky door. Artists aren't too particular about their surroundings. I mean, grab a glance at this place. Little pieces of dry clay stuck to the dusty floor. Bags of solid clay leaning against the wall, awaiting their transformation. Shelves lined with musty, heavy plastic—the perfect drying spot for the pottery. The messy, moist residue that lingers on the steel wheel where the potter works.

And feel the atmosphere of the studio. Cool, not cold. Warmth dries out the clay. The clay. Its unusual, earthy smell hangs in the air.

Oh, look. The potter is about to begin a new piece. Amazing. From a single lump of clay, he is about to create a masterpiece.

Watch as he throws the clay on the wheel, centering it perfectly. Observe how he uses his water-dipped hands to mold the shape he sees in the sketchbook of his mind. See how his fingers inside the pot gently push outward to give width to the middle of his creation. Then both hands around the clay press inward, narrowing the top of the piece. So purposeful! So artistic!

God works in the same way. He has created each one of us with great care. He has molded us with his loving hands into the shape that pleases his eye and fills his heart with pride.

Stop and think about it. Every part of you, from the top of your head down to the tip of your toes, was custom designed just for you in a way that delights your heavenly Father, the Ultimate Potter!

The psalmist David was well aware of this fact.

Picture the faithful shepherd boy, one star-filled night, plopped down amidst the roving sheep. See him contemplating the steady beating of his heart, the hardness of his fingernails, the prints on his palms, the softness of his skin, the connectedness of his veins that carry his life-giving blood.

In that precise moment when the reality of God's awesomeness burst in his heart, he joyously spoke to God saying,

> You made all the delicate, inner parts of my body, and knit them together in my mother's womb. Thank you for making me so wonderfully complex! It is amazing to think about. Your workmanship is marvelous—and how well I know it.   PSALMS 139:13-14 (TLB)

Did you catch that? Who did David say created and designed him? GOD! David realized only God was capable of creating him so incredibly! Do you? How much do you know about the awesome body God has knit together especially for you? Take this quiz and find out!

BODY QUIZ:
Fearfully and Wonderfully Made

1. The number of cells in your body is approximately:
   A. 500,000
   B. 100,000,000,000
   C. 75,000,000

2. The brain has four separate lobes, together weighing:
   A. 8 ounces
   B. 12 pounds, 7 ounces
   C. 3 pounds

3. The most common blood type is:
   A. O
   B. AB
   C. B negative

4. The kidneys' job is to:
   A. regulate fluid
   B. break down carbohydrates
   C. cleanse the blood

5. How many gallons of blood does the heart pump every day?
   A. 54
   B. 1800
   C. 364

6. The number of bones in the wrist and hand is:
   A. 30
   B. 17
   C. 9

7. The several dozen muscles in the face are capable of making
_____ different expressions:
   A. 7,000
   B. 22
   C. 106

8. A sneeze can exceed up to how many miles per hour?
   A. 54
   B. 2
   C. 100

9. The responsibility of the body's 50 billion white blood cells is
to:
   A. add protein
   B. attack invaders
   C. nourish the heart

10. Approximately how many colors can the 107,000,000 cells in
each eye distinguish?
   A. 1000
   B. 97
   C. 4050

Scoring:

How many did you get right? 1-B, 2-C, 3-A, 4-C, 5-B, 6-A, 7-A, 8-C, 9-B, 10-A.

Wow!

That's not all!

Did you know...

★ One square inch of skin has approximately 65 hairs, 100 oil-glands, 650 sweat glands, and 1,500 nerve receptors?

★ If your blood vessels were laid end to end they would circle around the globe... twice?

★ Your muscles produce enough heat to boil water for one hour?

★ Your inner ear contains as many circuits as the telephone system of a good-size city?

★ Your nose can detect between 4,000 and 10,000 different odors?

★ Your tongue has four types of taste buds: Sweet (on the tip), salty and sour (on the sides) and bitter (center, back)?

Wow! God has done an unbelievably fabulous job creating you!!

Now, check this out. What did David say in response to the way God made him? (Flip back a few pages to read the verse again).

Thank you!

Thank you?

Thank you!!! Have you ever looked in the mirror and rattled off a round of *thank yous* to God? Imagine it. "Thank you, Lord, for my narrow nose. Thank you for my sixty-seven moles. Thank you for the way my eyebrows arch. Thank you for my strong bones. Thank you for the muscles that give me strength."

Go ahead, give it a try! *Now?* Yep, now!

1. Thank you, Lord _____

   _____

   _____

2. Thank you, Lord _____

   _____

   _____

3. Thank you, Lord _____

   _____

   _____

4. Thank you, Lord _____

   _____

   _____

5. Thank you, Lord _____

   _____

   _____

Keep it up! Every time you peer into the mirror to blow-dry your hair or glide on some lip gloss, take time to thank God for YOU!

It may feel weird at first. Maybe even foolish. Perhaps you'll have to pry the words out of your mouth. Start with a whisper. It's OK!

Thanking God for your appearance may require you to take a new look at yourself. Get a fresh perspective. It may require you to be less judgmental of what you see in the mirror. Could it be that it's time for you to begin to see your facial features and your body as a gift from God?

Up Close and Personal
with "Little Person" Carey Posey

In P.E. she was almost always the last one chosen for team sports. When she needs to call her mom, she wonders if she will be able to reach the pay phone's coin slot. And bathrooms are a problem. She can't grasp the paper seat covers in the public restroom. She certainly hopes she doesn't get assigned to a top locker in art class. As a child she faced teasing from others and still today must endure their awkward stares.

Carey is unique. Her body is probably about half the size of yours. She stands all of 3'10" in her stocking feet. Dwarf height. She prefers to be called a "little person."

Over and over the cruel name calling and rejection from others would leave Carey in tears. Then the tears turned to anger toward God. "Why did you do this to me?" she seethed at her Maker.

One day at summer camp, Carey listened in on a seminar called "Worthy or Worthless?" The Lord used it to open her eyes and heart. "I began to understand that my body is a gift from God. Say a friend gave me a present for my birthday. I opened it and saw a pair of earrings, then pushed the gift back at her saying I didn't like them. I didn't want them. I realized that's what I was doing to God by not accepting his gift to me."

It took time, but Carey now sees her body as a different kind of gift, one that she can now thank God for. "I'm always glad that I didn't turn *away* from God in my anger," Carey says. In fact, she has allowed God to use her uniqueness in her life and the lives of others.

"I believe being a little person has developed my character. I am more understanding of other kids' struggles. I have also learned to look past the outer appearance and look for the good in each person's heart. I've been through teasing, several surgeries, physical limitations. Plus, I have been able to help others feel more grateful for what God has given *them*."

Carey has allowed her dwarfism to be a witness for Christ. "Other kids see I have peace in Christ. With him I know who I am, where I am coming from, and where I am going."

Carey's faith is the focus of her life. Because she sometimes feels left out of certain social situations, she chooses to use her time to study God's Word, pray, and memorize Scripture. Plus, she is an avid reader and loves to sew and to develop her skill as a writer (she is working on a series of children's books that she would love to have published some day).

If you met Carey today, obviously you would notice that she is a little person. You might even hear her jokingly refer to herself as "Micro Goddess" or "Short Stuff." But more importantly, you would notice her bright smile and friendly manner. Indeed, she has accepted the gift God has given her and is allowing him to use it for his special purposes, for his glory.

Who Has the Perfect Frame?

You may have heard of "Bodies by Jake" or "Bodies by Gilda." Well, you have a "Body by God." That's right. Head on back to Psalm 139! Check out verse 15:

My frame was not hidden from you when I
was made in the secret place.

PSALMS 139:15 (NIV)

Your *frame!* That's your body type. Your bone structure.

Of course, there are thousands of different body designs, but God created three main frames: Endomorph! Mesomorph! Ectomorph!

Endomorphs have large bones, tend to be broad across the shoulders and hips, and they are curvaceous—you know, they have the curves! Mesomorphs have medium-sized bones and tend to have greater muscular development and more strength than the other two. These are often the bodies of true athletes! The build of the ectomorph is narrow, with small bones and a small chest. (I am an ectomorph, small chest and all!)

Take a look around you. Notice that each frame you see has a few special features? Narrow shoulders with broad hips. Thin arms with thick ankles. Long legs with a short trunk (main body). Slim calves with large feet.

There are no right or wrong body types! Every body, *your* body, is constructed just the way God planned. (By the way, no amount of dieting or exercise can change your basic bone structure.)

Abby's wispy appearance is perfect for her favorite hobby: ballet!

Michelle's muscular build, with her square body frame, gives her the solid footing she needs to reach up and catch a pop fly into her glove, then make a quick pass to second base.

Lindsey's long, bony hands are part of what makes it possible for her to create harmonious melodies on her harp.

Everything about the way God designed you is not only perfectly pretty, it's part of his perfect plan.

Just like David and Carey, you can develop an attitude of gratitude toward your body—head to toe! You, too, can be thankful that a powerful, all-wise Being, greater than yourself, truly did stamp his seal of approval on you!

Yep. David knew he was God-designed. So are you. Still need more proof?

Check out God's surprise visit to Jeremiah. Young Jerry, who wasn't much older than you, was born into a family of priests. Well, one evening he was home studying the sanctuary manual by the light of the lantern—totally minding his own business—when God showed up and made this mind-boggling statement:

> Before I formed you in the womb I knew you.   JEREMIAH 1:5 (NAS)

Jeremiah must have shaken his head, cleared his ears, and let out a very intelligent, "Huh?"

But wait.

Let's look at this word by word.

The statement starts out, "Before I," meaning God!

"formed," meaning God's hand-crafting touch!

"you," that's Jeremiah!

"in the womb," that's where God did his designing!

"I knew you," meaning God had already mapped out Jeremiah's personality traits, temperament, likes and dislikes, strengths and weaknesses! PLUS, God had specific plans for Jeremiah even before he was conceived!

There you have it! God *himself* says that he formed and hand-crafted Jeremiah. Long before Jeremiah's folks ever thought of having a son, God had a plan to bring Jeremiah into the world. Jeremiah was GOD'S IDEA. God planned for him and designed him. He did the same for you! You were God's idea.

You may have been told you were a surprise. Perhaps you overheard someone say you were a mistake. Maybe someone said you were supposed to be a boy. NO WAY! Everything about your appearance, your personality, your gifts, and your talents, are God-given!

GIRL TALK
Are You Uniquely Attractive?

"Yes. Everything I have looks different from others, even my family members. That alone tells me I'm unique."

Emily, 16

"God says he made me in *his* image—therefore, I must be beautiful."

Kim, 14

"I struggle with my appearance whenever I see someone I think is cuter than me. I guess that's not fair to God, is it?"

Sally, 15

"Definitely unique! But not in a bad sense! I really like how I look."

Tara, 14

His Signature Touch

Just like the potter who handcrafts each piece of pottery with his unique skill and creativity, so God has crafted you.

Speaking of the potter, he is ready to do some handiwork on a pot that's been drying for awhile. The clay has to have the right amount of firmness for the potter to add the final touches.

Each tool that he uses adds to the decoration of the piece. Check out the wavy lines the jagged-edge tool creates. Notice the pattern produced when he presses the wooden stamp onto the semi-soft clay. See how delicate the edge appears when he pierces the clay, allowing light to pass through?

Fascinating. Of course, the greatest tool of the artist is his imagination. Only he can stare at a lump of clay, all the while picturing in his mind the finished product.

Hey, look. The potter is smiling. The piece is complete and perfect in his eyes. A unique expression of himself. Truly a work of art.

Have you ever pondered the fact that you are a unique expression of God? The way you are designed reveals another aspect of God's creativity. You are complete and perfect in his eyes. Yep. That includes your thick ankles, long neck, skinny legs, and crooked nose. You are his workmanship! The Bible confirms this tidbit of truth!

> For we are his workmanship, created in Christ Jesus. EPHESIANS 2:10 (KJV)

Workmanship means WORK OF ART!

I love that!

You and I are God's work of art! We each have his signature touch. We are different from each other. Yet we are both valuable creations, molded and decorated by the Master Designer. And we are equally attractive to our Father God.

Hello! Did you get that? I don't want you to miss the important truth in that last big sentence. Let's try it again. *We are equally attractive to our Father God!* Got it? Good! He's not sitting up there saying, "Oh she's a cutie," or "Whoops, I could have done better on her," or "Oh, yeah, that petite one is sweet, maybe a bit too short, but sweet!" He thinks we're all gorgeous! In fact, he's crazy about us. He made us!

He's the Ultimate Potter! Check out these words from the Holy Book:

> Oh, Lord, you are our Father.
> We are the clay, you are the potter;
> we are all the work of your hand.
>
> ISAIAH 64:8 (NIV)

The hands of your loving Heavenly Father have given you a natural beauty that is yours alone. A look of your own, straight from the Throne! *You are, without a doubt, a Babe! You've got the look!*

Up Close and Personal
with Recording Artist Lisa Bevill

"I'd pick up *Seventeen* magazine," Lisa remembers, "and just stare at supermodel Christie Brinkley. I wanted so badly to look like her."

You wouldn't guess just by looking at award-winning contemporary Christian recording artist Lisa Bevill that she was once frustrated and depressed over the "design" God had chosen for her!

"I hated my thighs, my stomach, everything about me. Christie was beautiful and popular, and I wanted what she had," Lisa shares.

With the help of a friend, Lisa realized that rejecting God's design for her was blinding her from seeing all the positive things about herself. When she looked closely, she saw she was full of potential!

"When I began to see myself through God's eyes instead of my own, the depression started to lift."

As the truth that God loved her exactly as she was began to blossom in her heart (after all, she was *his* idea!), Lisa started liking what she saw in the mirror's reflection. In fact, she actually looked at every part of her body and said, "You know what? I love you, and I'm gonna try to make you better than you are. But I'm not going to knock myself out trying to look like this month's cover girl."

Wise choice! Today, Lisa likes herself and feels content. She's using all God has given her to fulfill his dreams for her life. That, of course, includes singing his praises with that great voice!

(Adapted from "Lisa Bevill: A Christie Brinkley Wanna Be... Not Anymore," *Brio* magazine, September 1993)

Have you ever felt like Lisa? Ever struggled with accepting God's special design for you? Even though you know the Scriptures, do you look in the mirror and think, "Babe? No way!!"

Well, you're not alone! Sometimes we all find it hard to think of ourselves this way. There are lots of reasons for this. When we compare ourselves with others, or with the images in the media, we look in the mirror on our not-so-glorious days and say to ourselves, "You've got to be kidding me!"

Sometimes other people say things that get us to think this way. It can be that creepy boy across the street who yells "Crater-face" when you walk by. Maybe a popular girl in your English class makes snide comments about your clothes. Maybe there are even people in your *family*—who are supposed to love you no matter what—whose unthinking comments hurt you. This kind of "toxic teasing" can poison your self-confidence and stop you from seeing yourself as the positively awesome gal you truly are! If you'd like to learn how to "declaw" these catty remarks, then turn the page.

But first, if you have problem skin—or if you just want to keep your complexion looking nice—then here's a "Beauty Bonus" just for you!

BEAUTY BONUS
Sensible Steps to Great-Looking Skin

Take care of your special look through sensational skin care. In the morning and before bed, cleanse your face with a non-detergent bar or lotion cleanser. Work the sudsy lather in a circular motion. Rinse with lukewarm water; avoid extremes in temperature. Pat dry. Next, dab on astringent (or toner) with a 100 percent cotton ball. This will remove excess oil, slough off old skin cells, and shrink pores.

Finally, give your skin a drink with moisturizer. Unless you have very dry skin, oil-free types are best. Next, apply a sunscreen (SPF 15 or higher) to protect your skin from the sun's harmful rays. Top this routine off with six to eight glasses of water daily to add moisture from the inside out.

two

"Did You Hear What He Called Me?"
Tackling Toxic Teasing

*I*t happens to all of us at one time or another.

For me, it was in the eighth grade. I was babysitting for my neighbor, David, on a Saturday afternoon. We were riding our bikes over to the school playground, but to get there, we had to pedal past the home of the "terrible two." They were usually hanging out on their front porch, with a few of their high school buddies, boosting their egos.

I was truly scared of these guys. I didn't want them to see me. I panicked and prayed they would be busy rebuilding a car or pumping up their muscles for each other, but no. There they were!

In a strained whisper I started frantically encouraging little David to pedal faster and faster. With my eyeballs glued to the pavement, I was hoping the beastly boys wouldn't even notice us.

But I'm not that lucky.

They spotted us.

The studly, blond-haired one (he was a BMOC—big man on campus) hollered out, "Hey, Ardner" (that's my maiden name), "what happened to your face? Get run over by a truck?" (Gee, how original.)

OUCH. I wanted to die. Disappear. Poof, I'd be gone! I wanted to be like Elliot with E.T. and ride my bike off into the sky, never to be heard from again!

I certainly didn't feel attractive after being the object of a good laugh for that ruthless crew. (I didn't smell attractive either—I broke out in the biggest sweat.) I didn't like feeling that my appearance prompted such a rotten remark! Was it my octagon-shaped wire-rimmed glasses? Could my shiny silver braces be the cause? Maybe it was the cluster of pimples on my chin (ever notice how they like to appear in groups?).

How could they suggest my face looked like the result of a tragic encounter with a truck?

Recovering from such teasing can take a while! I remember the incident like it happened yesterday. Why? Because painful memories are hard to forget! When your emotions are tied into an incident, it is often logged into your memory bank for a lifetime.

(By the way, I just have to tell you this! Two years later, after I had blossomed into a babe as a sophomore, and the studly, blond-haired guy was a senior, he asked me out for a *date!* My response? *No way, buddy!*)

"What Do I Do When a Guy Teases Me?"

Being teased about your appearance hurts. It can make a perfectly happy gal suddenly feel insecure. Chrissy recently wrote to me about an encounter she had with some guys in the lunch line the first week of school.

Kevin, a boy she recognized from her biology class, walked up to her and said, "Hey, did you know you're a Pirate's Delight?"

Not knowing whether to smile or ignore him, Chrissy awkwardly shifted and said, "I am?"

"Yeah," Kevin continued, "you have a sunken chest." Kevin and his friends burst into laughter.

There was no way she could have braced herself for that zinger. Chrissy suddenly lost her appetite and left the cafeteria in tears.

Guys can be so cruel. Yet, the weird thing about it is that sometimes they tease because they *like* you!

Guys will often say unkind things to girls they are attracted to. They find it too intimidating to be honest about their feelings, especially if they are uncomfortable handling their emotions toward girls! Go figure!

And yet, teasing from guys can be most hurtful. Girls tease girls because they are jealous, spiteful, or just plain catty! We seem to be able to blow that off a bit more easily. Guys are a different story; girls tend to take their jesting to heart.

Try to remember that most of them are just puffing themselves up by poking fun at you. The trouble is, they don't know where to draw the line. Often they go too far!

In fact, they may even give you a nickname, inspired by one of your physical features. They like to pick on body parts! Growing up, I was always called bird legs, because of my skinny legs and knobby knees. Unfortunately, I fit other descriptions as well: four-eyes, metal-mouth, and freckle face!

GIRL TALK
Hey, What's Your Nickname?

"Hairball. I have tons of hair."   Gail, 14

"Giraffe Neck. My neck is so long."   Susie, 12

"Flatsy Patsy. Self-explanatory!"   Patsy, 15

"Bubble Butt. I have an athletic rear."   Jill, 16

> "Yoda. My ears always stick out." Michelle, 14
>
> "Mustache Mama. I have more hair on my lip than most of the guys my age." Kara, 13

Though guys, girlfriends, and family members just think they're being funny, nicknames are still unfair. I couldn't do anything about my skinny legs, just like you can't do anything about your pointed chin, tiny eyes, stubby toes, or whatever!

Nicknames should really be called *kicknames!* After all, that is exactly what they do—they kick us right where it hurts!

But don't despair! Some of your least favorite features may end up being your faves! They could just need some time to develop. Some of us have to "grow into" our final appearance.

Yep. All sorts of features you get teased about may change as you go through the Big P!

Plunging into Puberty

Puberty is that oh-so-special time in your life when everything seems to go wicky-wacky. Some parts of these changes might make you feel self-conscious at times. The good news is… these changes are a perfectly normal part of growing up. (Of course, if you have any questions or concerns, it's always a good idea to talk with a parent or your family doctor.) As your body changes and develops, your look will do the same!

Let's check out the process! Which of these have you experienced so far?

Growth spurts! During puberty your hormones come out of hibernation and your body grows at a faster rate as it changes from a little girl's into a young woman's body. (A guy's growth spurt and development is usually two years later than a girl's—that's why girls often tower over boys in the sixth through the ninth grades!) You'll notice that last year's khakis are up around your ankles, and those new Reeboks are suddenly too snug.

Bones lengthen! Your bones start growing longer and denser. And usually, not all at the *same* time! This accounts for those stages of awkwardness and lack of coordination that you will probably experience. Just sit tight! Everything will catch up!

Facial features change! Your jaw bone develops, making your face appear longer. Plus, your cheekbones widen. Both of these changes can affect your eye and nose areas, often working your face into its perfect proportions. Eventually, your face takes on a more mature look.

Here come the curves! Your pelvic bone widens and your hips and thighs fill out. Don't panic! You're not getting fat! God intended for the female body to be fleshy so that you'll be ready for having babies (later in life—after you're married!). Obviously, those who would tease girls about teenage weight gain are ignorant of God's plan.

Menstrual cycle moves into action! Your "female" hormones (estrogen, progesterone, and follicle stimulating and luteinizing hormones) take flight. Your period begins. The number of days it lasts each month and the intensity of the blood flow vary from girl to girl. Cramps? Some girls get them; some don't. (Get the full scoop in Susie Shellenberger's book, *What You've Always Wanted to Know About Your "."*)

Breasts blossom! OK, here you go! Your nipples push out from your chest as your breasts begin to swell and blossom, sometimes one faster than the other! It can be an uncomfortable time when you're too big for Band-Aids and too small for a real bra! But fear not. You'll fill out a "cup" soon enough. To avoid embarrassing "nipple" moments, select a bra with a thicker cup lining (not padded, but not single-layered).

Hair happenings! Soft hair appears on various areas of your body: under your arms and in the pubic area as well as on your chest and upper lip. You may even grow hair between your eyebrows! The hair on your legs and arms usually darkens during this time as well. Don't worry... all this is *normal.* (Note: Don't try to shave facial hair! If your facial hair is really dark, try a bleaching cream that is specially formulated for facial hair. Or go to a salon and have the hair waxed away. Absolutely *avoid* products that claim to "dissolve" hair!)

Palms perspire! Your sweat glands get into gear and start pumping out perspiration at a faster and perhaps more intense rate. Though some girls sweat more than others, it's all part of the big P! Arm yourself with a daily dose of underarm protection!

Oozing oil glands! Your skin produces more oil, which often contributes to blackheads, whiteheads, and pimples. Oil production usually tapers off in the late teens.

All of these changes are totally normal. Absolutely natural. They are part of the unbelievably complex, ingenious Masterminded workings of the human body.

As you travel down the puberty path, you will come into your look! Some of your less appealing qualities are often only temporary! It's true. Those picked-on features of yours may become your prized possessions.

Get this. I told you I was always called "bird legs" as a kid, even as a teen. Well, when I was eighteen I won the Miss Keystone Lake Pageant. I was so excited as I prepared for the

Miss Oklahoma Pageant. I exercised faithfully and practiced my poise and walking techniques. Every night I could be heard plucking out the tune of my classical guitar piece until my performance was near perfection.

I was thrilled to be named second runner-up (well, OK, I was a bit upset I didn't win), but this is my favorite part.

The second night of the pageant I was in the preliminary swimsuit competition. I won! These ol' bird legs nailed the swimsuit award and a $3,000 college scholarship!

I love it!! I guess those miserable months in braces that gave me this straight-toothed smile were an asset, too! *And,* my long, thin fingers made it possible for me to play the classical guitar as well as I did!

After all, God *does* have a reason for designing us the way he did!

Up Close and Personal
with 1995 Brio Girl Cari Fallin

Cari Fallin, selected from over two thousand applicants by *Brio* magazine to be the 1995 Brio Girl, has this to say about one of her unique features.

"I'm very petite, but I have really big feet! I have grown accustomed to them by realizing that everything God does has a purpose, even though I may not see what that purpose is! Besides, my mom keeps reminding me that my feet provide a good foundation for me to stand on!"

Be patient. Give your look time to develop.

"The Ugly Duckling," a Hans Christian Andersen fairy tale, illustrated this point perfectly. You probably read it as a child.

Allow me to refresh your memory.

The mother duck, which we'll call Mrs. D, had diligently sat on her nest of eggs waiting expectantly for the happy hatching day to arrive. It finally did. All was well as the tiny ducklings pecked their way out of the shells. That is, until the largest egg's duckling pecked through, peeked out, then popped open his shell. Uh-oh. There was something different about this guy. He was big. He was gray. He was U-G-L-Y! He was quickly quacked right out of Duckville by his family and neighboring ducksters, just because he didn't look exactly like the other ducklings.

After a long, hard winter of shivering alone in the snow and fending for himself, springtime appeared. And so did a new and improved duckling. The big, gray bird had become a beautiful swan! He could barely believe the reflection he saw in the cool, blue pond! The ugly duckling had matured into a sensational swan. In fact, his new flock of friends were so taken by his beauty, they bowed before him!

OK, it doesn't happen to this degree for all of us, but you get the point!

Unfortunately, I'll bet some of you can identify more with being quacked out of Duckville than with discovering a new-looking you! Maybe you are suffering from toxic teasing and the painful put-downs from family, friends, or maybe a guy you were hoping to impress? Hurts, doesn't it?

The good news is this: There are things you can do to "manage" the toxic teasing so it doesn't poison your system. First let's look at the teasing that hits closest to home!

What If Your Parents Are Teasing You?

Those folks you call mom and dad (perhaps stepmom or stepdad for some of you) can have a powerful effect on you by arranging the twenty-six letters of the alphabet into words that "sting" your heart when they land on your ears! No doubt you've experienced the pain of parents' hurtful comments. We all do to some degree.

Unfortunately, many times your parents are unaware of how their remarks are affecting you. Their teasing might just be their way of giving you attention. Or perhaps they think their statements made in jest will motivate you to change in some way.

Sounds sort of backward, doesn't it? Rather than being straight and genuine, parents sometimes tease as a way of communicating a message. They use teasing talk in hopes of getting you to do something that they think will be good for you. They love you!

Yet, it is absolutely acceptable and most often absolutely necessary that you admit to yourself (and to your folks) that their words hurt. Stuffing your feelings will only cause them to ooze out in other ways. So, be brave and acknowledge your feelings. When you do this, it will help you to move on to some constructive ways of handling the poking and teasing!

For instance, let's say you come home from school and walk into the kitchen. There on the table is a plate of fresh-baked brownies that your mother made for dinner. As you reach for one, she says to you: "You don't really need to add that brownie to your blubber butt, do you?"

What do you do?

★ Say to yourself, "She should talk," and defiantly take a huge bite. Then turn around, stalk out of the room, and refuse to look at her for the rest of the day.

★ Turn around and leave the room before she can see your tears. Then refuse both dinner *and* the brownie that night. Resolve to put yourself on a strict diet until your hips disappear.

★ Yell hysterically at your mother, *"You* should talk. If you didn't want us to eat these things, why did you make them in the first place?"

★ Calmly say to your mother, "Ouch, Mom. 'Blubber Butt'? I didn't realize you thought about me that way. Why did you say that?"

If you picked the last option, good for you! The thing is, parents really DO care about your health and well-being. They love you! They want the best for you—they just might have a cock-eyed way of showing it. Here are a couple of things you can do to take the sting out of these offhanded comments:

BE PATIENT

Your parents are only human! We all say things we regret later. If someone says something to you that hurts your feelings, give him or her the benefit of the doubt. Remember the Golden Rule: "Do unto others as you would have them do unto you." Give the other person the same forgiveness you would want him or her to give to you if *you* messed up!

ASK YOURSELF: IS THERE SOME TRUTH IN WHAT WAS SAID?

Maybe it wasn't delivered in the nicest possible way, but there may be a message hidden in that comment.

Perhaps you could try asking the person who made that hurtful comment exactly what he or she was trying to say... (just keep your tone of voice sincere, *not* sassy!). The last response above, "Ouch, Mom. 'Blubber Butt'?" gives the "messenger" a chance to clarify what she meant by that remark. Maybe she's worried that you'll have the same weight problem *she's* always wrestled with. Maybe she's worked hard that day and feels unappreciated, and regretted saying what she did as soon as the words were out of her mouth (that's where the forgiveness part comes in). Maybe the grocery bills are going through the roof, and she's upset that your snacking is going to mess up her careful meal planning. Try to put yourself in her shoes.

PRAY FOR THE PERSON WHO HURT YOU

"What?!? You want me to *pray* for her?" Yep. Here's why. Breathing a quick prayer will help you to stay calm and respectful as you're talking to Mom or Dad. And if you don't like the outcome of your conversation, praying for the person who hurt you will keep your hurt from turning into resentment, which can build into bitterness. And bitterness is the *ultimate* toxin to your self-esteem!

Tips for Tackling Other Types of Teasing

OK, we've talked about how to handle parental teasing. But sometimes other people make comments, too—people who don't love you as much as your parents do. How can you deal effectively with the sting of hurtful talk? You need a plan of defense! Try this:

WRITE IT DOWN!

Bottling up your fractured feelings can lead to an emotional explosion! So, start by letting it all out in a journal. Record exactly what you feel and why you feel that way.

TALK IT OUT!

Share your feelings with a mature Christian friend, trusted youth leader, or parent. Sometimes just talking about it helps a ton. Plus, when you share your burden with a friend, it suddenly appears smaller.

PUT IT IN PERSPECTIVE!

Consider the source before you take their teasing to heart!
1. Who is the teaser? What position does he or she play in your life? Is it someone who has your best interests at heart?
2. Does this person know you well enough to have the right to share his or her opinion? (A close friend who cares about you should be taken more seriously than someone you don't know well, or whom you are trying to impress.)
3. Is this comment about you fact or fiction?
4. Even if there is truth in the teasing (so, maybe you *are* a frizzhead), is it really worth falling apart over?

LET IT GO!

Now we're getting down to the tough stuff!

When you choose to hold a grudge, it only hurts you! Jesus teaches us to forgive, no matter how much it hurts, no matter if the person deserves forgiveness or not. When you forgive others, you are being obedient to the Lord! He will honor that!

Think of yourself as choosing to "walk" in forgiveness. Walking is a continuous action. If you stop walking, you are standing!

Walking is continuous. That suggests that we are to continually forgive others. Plus, walking is a forward motion! So, let go of the hurt of the past and move forward!

SEEK PEACE, NOT REVENGE!

Another biggie! The Lord instructs us to be at peace with others, even to go so far as to love our enemies and pray for those who persecute us (find it in Matthew 5:44).

That's not all. Check out 1 Peter 3:8-9 (TLB).

> You should be like one big happy family, full of sympathy toward each other, loving one another with tender hearts and humble minds. Don't repay evil for evil. Don't snap back at those who say unkind things about you. Instead, pray for God's help for them, for we are to be kind to others, and God will bless us for it.

You can do it, with the Holy Spirit's help!

LEAN ON THE LORD!

Once you forgive and seek peace and blessings on those who have hurt you, the Lord will heal that hurt.

Sometimes he'll heal you all at once, sometimes in stages. Either way, lean on the Lord to pour his healing ointment out on you. He knows life is hard and that hurtful things happen. He is there to heal your brokenness.

That's why one of his names is Jehovah Rapha. That is the Hebrew term for "the God who heals." Go to him when your heart is bruised and your esteem is battered. He will make it better! I promise! I would never *tease* you about that!

You Are a One-of-a-Kind Design!

Though teasing "kicknames" may *attempt* to affect the way we feel about our appearance, they will only beat us down if we let them!

We each have a *choice* either to accept or reject God's design for us. Remember, God is the potter, we are the clay! Romans 9:20 in the Living Bible says, "Who are you to criticize God? Should the thing made say to the one who made it, 'Why have you made me like this?'"

You are the clay in the hands of God, the Potter.

His fingers formed and molded you according to his plan. If you asked God, "But what about the things I don't like about my appearance? These things that people tease me about? What about all these flaws?"

God would say in a gentle and loving tone, "Oh, no. You have no flaws. There are no defects in your appearance. Those features are the intricate *details* I have given only to you, to make you *one-of-a-kind!*"

You don't have defects, you have DETAILS!

Read that again, letting it soak in!

The details in your appearance are the handiwork of the Potter's tools. They are the decorations, designs, finishing touches that make you one-of-a-kind. You are a designer original!

Here's another news flash:

There Is No One Else Exactly Like You!

That's the honest truth!

Snag a look at this line-up:

★ No one has your exact thumb print.

★ No one has a "beauty mark" in the same place you do.

★ No one laughs just like you do.

★ No one has a little toe shaped exactly like yours.

★ No one has the same abilities and talents that you do.

★ No one has the same flecks of color in her pupil.

★ No one has a belly button shaped exactly like yours.

★ No one has your imagination—or your dreams!

★ Now that you've got your brain in gear, list five more of *your* very own, one-of-a-kind features!

1.

2.

3.

4.

5.

Are you catching on?

Are you convinced you are special?

It's true! **There will never be another you.**

I hope you are getting excited about yourself! You are definitely not a carbon copy or a computer-created clone. As you see yourself through God's eyes—from the Potter's perspective—you *can* learn to love and appreciate your unique design. Don't let anything—a playful joke, a jabbing jest, a low grade, a dress that's too small, shoes that seem to have shrunk, a clumsy stumble, or anything else—keep you from seeing your true God-given beauty!

BEAUTY BUSTER
J-J-J-Jealousy

One thing that will zap the beautiful smile from your face and cause a nasty wrinkle between your brows is jealousy. You know, that hostile way you feel when you think someone has something they don't deserve, but *you do!* It could be new clothes, a late curfew, good grades, or a steady boyfriend. Maybe it's their patient attitude or the ability to forgive that turns you green with envy.

Being jealous is actually being covetous. The Big Ten tell us not to covet (check out Exodus 20:17), which means to strongly desire something that belongs to someone else. Instead, with God's help we can learn to rejoice at the good fortune of others! We can be glad for others' achievements and special abilities. And with God's assistance our joy won't be fake! We can act from sincere hearts. Plus, we can grow to appreciate what God has or has not given to us! Think about it. If you stop looking "over the fence" at what others possess, you can focus on the wonderful things *you* possess. Having an attitude of gratitude is evidence that you've put the jealousy monster in its place!

BEAUTY BONUS
Accessorize with a Smile!

Want to know how to dress up your wardrobe without spending a dime? Care to discover the ONLY way to improve your looks without wearing makeup?

It's simple. Put on a SMILE.

Smiling brightens your eyes, adds a pleasant expression to your face, and perfectly accessorizes *any* outfit. Smiling adds a touch of beauty that you can't buy in a bottle or squeeze out of a tube!

Smiles can do more than improve your appearance. They can improve your relationships. Just think how your life would change if you smiled at your mom while you set the table or dried the dishes. What if your dad caught you grinning while you dusted the house or helped him rake the leaves? Talk about shock! Your parents would begin to see you in a whole new light! Your happy attitude would show a more mature you! That'll increase your trust factor and put a smile on Mom and Dad's faces, too! And all you have to do is put on a smile.

The Bible instructs us to put on a few other things as well. Listen up:

And so, as those who have been chosen of God, holy and beloved, put on a heart of compassion, kindness, humility, gentleness and patience; bearing with one another, and forgiving each other, whoever has a complaint against anyone; just as the Lord forgave you, so also should you. And beyond all these things put on love, which is the perfect bond of unity.

COLOSSIANS 3:12-14 (NAS)

A smile is the first step to putting on each of these things! A genuine smile communicates compassionate caring, true kindness, and a humble attitude. Turning up the corners of your mouth also shows you are patient, gentle, and that you are not holding a grudge! Most important, putting on a smile is proof of a heart that is full of love. That's a heart that is *beautiful!*

So, go ahead. Every day, every hour, every moment. Put it on! The most beautiful people in the world are those who smile!

three

"If Only I Looked Like Her!"
Overcoming the Comparison Trap

*W*ishing you looked like someone else is a snare that leads you right into a trap—the comparison trap! Before that cage door slams shut on you, consider what happened in Heidi's life (Heidi is the basically brilliant editor of this book!):

Have you ever wished you looked more like one of your friends? I did, when I was in seventh grade. Her name was Emma. She was a year older and I really looked up to her. Her long blonde hair flowed softly down her back, while my mousy brown mop always straggled in my eyes. Emma's mother allowed her to wear eye makeup—something my own mother absolutely forbade. Emma was an "early bloomer," and even in eighth grade she had curves in all the right places. I had curves in all the *wrong* places—and huge feet to boot!

Emma's beauty made me feel ugly. Her fashion sense reminded me how hopelessly out-of-date my own clothes were. She was graceful and outgoing; I tripped over my own two feet. Around Emma I felt like a four-eyed, metal-mouthed chunk. At first she tried to help me improve my appearance, but it made me mad because I never felt like I could measure up to her. Eventually we stopped being friends. Frankly, I never thought she'd notice my absence. Emma was very popular, especially with the boys.

Years later, I ran into Emma again. She reminded me of what had happened between us in junior high. Then she said something that I will never forget: "You know, Heidi, I was really jealous of you back then. You were so much smarter than me, and so much better in school." I couldn't believe it—all that time *she* had been jealous of *me!* It was so sad. We robbed ourselves of precious years of friendship—for no good reason!

Comparison Calamities

Comparing yourself to others can lead to only one of these two attitudes—both of them are risky!

"SO-AND-SO'S BETTER THAN ME!"

Have you or your friends made comments like this?

★ "If only I had Kelly's graceful legs."

★ "Can you believe how long Sara's nails are? Mine refuse to grow at all."

★ "I'd die to be Maggie's bra size. I've barely started to sprout."

★ "Did Carlee show you her new mascara? She's so lucky to have those beautiful lashes."

★ "I wish I had Lori's thick hair instead of this thin, stringy stuff."

★ "If I had a body like Peggy's, I'd have a boyfriend, too."

When measuring yourself up against others leaves you feeling blue, you are headed straight toward the inferiority pit! Ooh, not a pretty place to be! If you view yourself as less attractive, less important, or less valuable than others, you will end up being less than your best!

Don't let it happen!

Thinking you are mediocre compared to others will hold you back from becoming all God has planned for you to be!

It also makes it tough to apply Jesus' instructions to love others as yourself. First, you *have* to love *yourself,* including your short lashes, flat chest, stringy hair, big lips, knobby knees, and all! Remember, in Christ we are going for loved and forgiven, not perfection!

"I'M BETTER THAN SO-AND-SO!"

The second disastrous attitude is rarely spoken out loud. Instead, these comparisons ring in the hallways of your mind. Have you had similar thoughts to these, or sensed them in a friend?

★ "Kristy doesn't look nearly as hot in her cheerleading uniform as she thinks she does. My skirt fits a lot better than hers."

★ "Misty's haircut is hysterical. I'd never be so stupid as to try that style."

★ "My skin is so smooth, it hardly ever breaks out. Glad I'm not Sarah. She looks polka-dotted!"

★ "My chest isn't as big as Jill's, but I have great legs. Hers are dumpy."

★ "Cindy thought an 87 was a good score on the history final. What a joke. I got a 94."

If you see that you or a special gal-pal are rocking on the edge of the better-than-you baloney beam, beware! Thinking you are superior to others may leave you standing at the top... ALONE!

Yep. You can't fool your friends, family, and classmates. A puffed-up, egotistical, big-headed attitude is easy to detect. It will show up in the way you constantly check your reflection, insist on shopping at the "right" stores, and obsess over every outfit!

Having an inflated, boastful view of yourself will make a few of the Lord's commands tough on you, too. Let's see: Put others first. Be a servant. Don't think more highly of yourself than you ought. When you boast, boast only in the Lord. Hmm...

It's tempting to compare, but challenge yourself and your friends to put a halt to it! It's time to stop longing to look like someone else and comparing all the time and be thankful for who God made us to be.

Better yet, **let's celebrate!**

Comparing will only rob you of the ability to celebrate *your* look and encourage your friends to celebrate theirs, too!

GIRL TALK
What Is Your Most Celebrated Feature?

"My full lips." Trisha, 16

"My bushy hair—I'll never be bald!" Sue, 13

"Definitely my narrow fingers." Rachel, 16

"Believe it or not, my wide nose!" Anna, 14

"The mole on my cheek. I call it my beauty mark." Kath, 17

Your turn! What is *your* favorite feature?

_____

_____

_____

Unfortunately, some girls take concern for their looks too far and develop an obsession about their physical appearance! They spend so much time fixing their hair, clothes, and makeup that they miss the whole point of appreciating their *natural* beauty.

How about you? Do you obsess about your appearance so much that you neglect those inner qualities? Or could it be that you're neglecting your appearance? Stringy hair and chewed-up fingernails won't enhance your inner beauty, either. Balance is the key!

Are you perfectly balanced when it comes to taking care of your appearance? Let's find out!

BEAUTY QUIZ
Are You Obsessed with Your Appearance?
CIRCLE THE NUMBER THAT BEST DESCRIBES YOU!

1. The zit breaking out on your nose makes you feel self-conscious all day.

   5   **4**   **3**   **2**   **1**

   EEKS! OF COURSE!   SORT OF, BUT NOT A BIG DEAL.   NO WAY!

2. You change your outfit several times almost every day before heading off to school.

   5   **4**   **3**   **2**   **1**

   THAT'S ME!   WELL, SOMETIMES.   WHAT GOES ON, STAYS ON!

3. You planned on doing your makeup on the way to school. You discover your mascara is home in your cabinet. You:

5	**4**	**3**	**2**	**1**
BORROW IT!		FEEL NAKED.		LAUGH IT OFF!

4. Your best friend showed up at a party in a great dress that looked fab on her. You were:

5	**4**	**3**	**2**	**1**
VERY JEALOUS.		DETERMINED TO GET ONE, TOO!	GLAD SHE LOOKED NICE!	

5. It's a bad-hair day. Each strand protests the look you want. You're so frustrated, you end up crying!

5	**4**	**3**	**2**	**1**
PASS THE TISSUE!		KEEP TRYING.		GET REAL!

6. You love wearing Passion Pink lipstick, but notice all the mags are showing Fire Engine RED. You switch!

5	**4**	**3**	**2**	**1**
YOU BET!		MAYBE.		NOPE. PINK IT IS!

7. On an average morning, it takes you longer than 30 minutes to do your hair and make-up.

5	**4**	**3**	**2**	**1**
ALWAYS!		NOT QUITE.		NOPE!

8. A girl in your science class dropped fifteen pounds and had three dates in the last month. You start feeling pudgy and decide to skip lunch.

5	**4**	**3**	**2**	**1**
LUNCH & DINNER!		FELT FAT, BUT ATE.		HAPPY AS I AM!

Scoring

NOW ADD UP THE NUMBERS YOU CIRCLED
TO FIND YOUR TOTAL SCORE.

29 - 40 POINTS: Uh, oh! You are definitely obsessed! It's time to step back and stop making beauty such a high priority!

17 - 28 POINTS: Ask yourself: are there some areas in your life where you are overly concerned about your looks?

8 - 16 POINTS: Way to go! You seem to have a healthy perspective on beauty!

***

How did you do?

What did you learn about yourself? Are you ready to toss up the confetti and celebrate YOU?

I hope so!

By now, you have figured out that everyone has something about them that is beautiful, something worth celebrating.

But that's not the message you catch from magazines and movies. When was the last time you saw an actress wake up in the morning with drool on her chin and pillowcase, sleep crusted in the corners of her eyes, her hair matted down, sporting a totally makeup-free face? *Never!* Her lips are perfectly lined and glossed, her mascara is never smudged, and her hair is perfectly in place. Drool? Forget it. Not in a trillion years.

Society judges the physical attractiveness of a person on whether they possess all of the characteristics that *it* says are necessary to be considered beautiful! (Stay tuned, more on this in chapter four.)

How unfair!

Besides, isn't there more to beauty than physical perfection?
You bet there is!

What Is True Beauty?

Your study buddy, ol' Webster, fills us in on the facts about
real beauty. Check these out!

Beauty is:

★ The quality in a person or thing that gives "pleasure to the
senses"!

★ That which "positively stirs a person's emotions"!

★ That which "pleasurably exalts the mind or spirit"!

★ An "excellent quality"!

Beauty obviously includes a whole lot more than physical
appearance! Let's go a step further and check out some real
synonyms for *beautiful.* Perhaps we'll gain additional insight.

Here they are:

- Personable!
- Divine!
- Magnificent!
- First-Rate!
- Blessed!

- Pleasant!
- Excellent!
- Rare!
- Strong!

Wow!

Beauty applies to things that make us happy, give us joy, bring
smiles to our faces, and tears to our eyes! Things that are beautiful stir our emotions, like the thrill of winning a championship
game and the whole team hugging or the way you feel saying
good-bye to a special friend who is moving away.

Beautiful people are those who are friendly and put you at
ease. They are strong in character, have their mind set on the
divine, and bless others with what they do and say.

GIRL TALK
What Things Do You Think Are Awesomely Beautiful?

"A big bouquet of tulips. They are absolutely my favorites."

Betsy, 15

"When someone gives up something for someone else."

Lea, 14

"I think it's beautiful when I have a problem and my parents really listen and understand." Abby, 16

"Sitting on the deck with my whole family, watching the sun set on the lake. The colors and the calmness are awesome." Mary, 14

"A person with a beautiful attitude, a beautiful spirit, and a beautiful personality. These types of beauty are most important because physical beauty doesn't last."

Michelle, 17

"Someone who spends a lot of time in the Word and applies the truths learned to her life. That's beautiful."

Ann, 18

"When our entire soprano section is together and on key! We sound great!" Lori, 15

Your turn! What do *you* think is *beautiful?*

Lots of things are beautiful. Obviously, different stuff is beautiful to different people. Yet, what we've definitely discovered is that beauty is *more* than physical perfection!

Ever wonder what guys would consider beautiful? Well, just for you, I asked a few. Here's a peek into their opinions!

GUY TALK
Hey There, Boys, What's Beauty to You?

"The perfect lay-up shot."	Paul, 14
"The fog hanging over the duck pond."	Tim, 15
"A wedding ceremony."	Jordan, 16
"Seeing my parents hold hands."	Mark, 15
"Acing my chemistry exam."	Josh, 15

Not too wordy, but powerful! Now you have a bit of insight into these hard-to-figure creatures called guys.

OK, back to beauty…

We live in a world that is obsessed with looking perfect according to its own standards. We're surrounded, trapped in the world's beauty bubble!

Christians are not exempt from the pressure to look like a cover girl. I know I don't have to tell you that. Teens have it the toughest. They are the targets! This is the time of life when personal identity is largely tied to fitting in and belonging.

BEAUTY QUIZ:
What Is Your Highest Priority?

In this obsessed world it can be easy to get your priorities mixed up, and start to major on the minors. Let's see how you're doing!

Rank the following from 1 (most important) to 10 (least important):

☐ My clothes

☐ My abilities

☐ My personality

☐ My face

☐ My hair

☐ My grades

☐ My health

☐ My relationship with God

☐ My body

☐ My friendships

I hope your relationship with God, your friendships, your health, and your personality ranked near the top!

You can choose not to play by society's high, impossible standards. Why give society the power to rob you of the ability to feel good about the way God designed you? Why judge yourself unfairly? Why compare when you can celebrate? It won't be easy to change your focus, but with Christ's help, you can do it, step by step.

You can start by readjusting the way you look at beauty. This article from *Campus Life* magazine makes that point pretty clear:

All the Beautiful People

Ever notice how many beautiful people there are? Most people are startlingly attractive. Ideally proportioned. Stunningly outfitted with class and style. Most women exude a luscious sensuality that stirs wild impulses in striking male hunks (most guys). These perfect people who surround us smile alluringly, revealing straight white teeth and igniting, sparkling, fluid eyes. The guys flex, and firm muscles ripples under chic sweaters, which impresses perfect females who are round and ample, lean and lithe, in all the right places. Most people are beautiful. I know. I read magazines. Watch television. Catch an occasional movie. Glance at billboards. Obviously, most people are beautiful.

Ever notice how few beautiful people there are? Few are startlingly attractive. Ideally proportioned. Stunningly outfitted with class and style. Not too many women are round and ample, lean and lithe in all the right places. Few exude a luscious sensuality that stirs wild impulses in firm-muscled male hunks. (There aren't too many of those, either.)

Most people are less than beautiful.

I know. I've sat in the school's bleachers, observed the student body filing in for a game. I have sat in bus stations or airline terminals and simply observed people. I have noticed those who stand in line in supermarkets or department stores. I've been to the beach. How many beautiful people are there? Few.

And even most of the beautiful would point to imperfections, minute or mammoth, that rob them of the security of feeling beautiful.

Ever notice what high standards we set for ourselves? We have defined attractiveness so restrictively that we have excluded most people. Ourselves included. Ourselves excluded. You must be just the right height and weight and complexion. With just the right foot size, nose size, tooth size, lip size, thigh size. We have created a narrow band of beauty. Most of us are outside its limits.

So why do we define beauty with such tight confines? Why can't we observe the wonder of the human body—and the population's diversity!—and call everyone beautiful? Why must beauty be rare before we will consider it beautiful?

I have read of a city where beauty is commonplace. Roadways are not simply plated, but paved with gold. Walls are inlaid with jewels. Could we tolerate this city? Or would we shield our eyes from such glinting grandeur as we searched for a rare lump of asphalt or a square of linoleum?

To us, gold and jewels are valuable because they are rare. If they were commonplace, we would take them for granted as valueless. Were we dropped into a world of plentiful diamonds, we'd give granite engagement rings.

Such an ingrained idea (beauty must be rare) drives us to define beauty so exclusively that most of us are left out.

Ever notice that standards of beauty change from culture to culture, from year to year? One group values an ivory complexion. Another goes for hide tanned under the summer sun (or winter heat lamp). One culture tattoos the face, pierces the nose, or slips discs under the lips to enlarge them. Another repaints the face an "embarrassed pink" and pierces the earlobe—once, twice, three times. One group tightly braids the hair, another frees the locks to cascade over the shoulders and down the back. A wet look. A dry look. Heads bushy. Heads shaved. Individually and together we have the ability to choose our definition of beauty. And we do choose it. We alter it to follow shifting fads (though we keep the limits of attractiveness painfully narrow).

Perhaps it's time to redefine beauty, to give it a broader definition. Maybe physical perfection shouldn't be so restrictive. Maybe we should develop a bit more tolerance for our own appearance and the appearance of others. What would happen if we did? Would we discover physical beauty where we never guessed it existed? And, our preoccupation with physical things diminished, would we suddenly see a beauty that had little to do with things physical?

Ever notice how many beautiful people there are? All of us!

("All the Beautiful People," *Campus Life* magazine, January 1992). Used by permission.

Yes, we are all beautiful. In the eyes of society? No. In the eyes of God? Yes. Ephesians 1:6 (KJV) says we are "accepted in the beloved"! Christians and those who love Jesus are accepted and are children of God.

God's stamp of approval and his acceptance of you are far more precious than the big OK from society. Plus, God's approval of you is lasting. It won't change. You can count on it. Depend on it. Trust it.

God is not obsessed with physical appearance. He desires for us to be obsessed with only one thing. It's not the *look*. It's HIM!

Why waste valuable time wishing you looked like someone else? Don't allow comparisons to blind you from seeing all the wonderful things about yourself, all the things worth celebrating!

What did you say? You believe God has given you a special beauty, but when you see the cover of *Sassy* or *YM*, you don't *feel* very pretty?

That's called MEDIA MANIPULATION!
Go get a soda, come back, and check out chapter four!

BEAUTY BUSTER
A Sneaky Heart

It happened at K-Mart. I had been dying to wear make-up, but my parents put a firm foot down on that one. Yet, there it was: the cosmetics aisle. I strolled among the foundations and eye shadows, longing to own some of my own. Then I saw it. A basket of blushes! And the best part? They were on sale! A mere fifty cents stood in the way of my owning "Radiant Rose."

I had the money.

But where was Mom? That was the key question. I strained to catch a glimpse of her. There she was! Way over in housewares. If I was quick, I could do it. She would never know! Or so I thought.

I tried to keep my elated emotions under control on the drive home. I didn't want her to suspect!

I safely concealed the blush in the side pocket of my navy book bag. The next morning, just before first period bell rang, I strutted out of the girls' bathroom making my first appearance in living color! I was finally wearing blush! And Mom and Dad didn't know!

At least not the first few days. But Friday was doomsday. As usual, Mom picked me up from school. The horrified look on her face could only mean one thing. *I forgot to wash the blush off!* My plan had worked perfectly until that moment. I was caught red-handed—red-cheeked, actually!

I handed over the Radiant Rose, knowing I had a lot of explaining to do. My parents trusted me to obey them, but I chose to go it alone and sneak the blush behind their backs.

How far would you go for beauty? What might you do to wear clothes or makeup your parents say are off-limits?

Is fitting in, wearing the latest lipstick, or showing up in a tight-ribbed top really worth deceiving the people who *really* matter?

Take it from someone who knows. The answer is NO!

It is far better to make the effort to openly discuss these things with your parents until you can reach an agreement. Without raising your voice, being snippy or pouting, do your best to dig until you discover the reasons *why* they feel the way they do (body-tight clothes, low-cut tops, thick black mascara... all of these things can send messages that you might miss but your parents understand).

Calmly share your views, then pray together.

Perhaps you can reach a few compromises. For instance, clear mascara doesn't give you full, thick-look lashes, but it does add a glossy shine that your folks might feel more comfortable with. Deep or bright-colored lipsticks freak out most fathers, but a tinted gloss in soft pink or peach might be the thing that satisfies both of you!

You may have heard the saying, "What they don't know, won't hurt them." But it's not true. Deceiving your parents hurts them—and *you!* Don't do it. Talk it out. Be patient.

Show you are mature and ready to be trusted by honoring their decisions.

What do you get out of the deal? A peaceful, loving relationship that is based on mutual respect and trust. Believe me, that's far better than any ol' blush!

four

More Than Barbie!

Mastering Media Manipulation

There is a very subtle yet powerful force at work in our world today. It is trying to control what we do and what we believe, especially about beauty and the possibility of attaining physical perfection.

You guessed it—it's the media!

The media portrays images of beauty that can affect the way we feel about ourselves, if we aren't careful.

The voice of Madison Avenue is very forceful, often in an underhanded way.

Slick advertising slogans slip into our subconscious, embed themselves in our brains. The scary part is that we usually aren't aware of it.

Any chance you're a victim without realizing it?

Let's test it!

Read the following slogans and see if you can fill in the blanks and list the name of the product.

SLICK SLOGANS GUESS-LIST

Slick Slogans	Product

1. Redefining beautiful _____

2. Maybe she's born with it, maybe it's_____

3. Before you dress,_____

4. Kiss a little longer _____

5. Just do it _____

CHECK YOURSELF: 1. Cover Girl; 2. Maybelline; 3. Caress; 4. Big Red; 5. Nike.

See how clever those catchy little tunes and phrases are? They were right there on the tip of your tongue! I'll bet you didn't even realize you knew most of these slogans by heart.

It's proof that commercials, radio jingles, advertisements, and magazine ads absolutely have the power to influence. They may even affect us in an obvious way!

I fell prey when I was your age.

Seventeen. YM. Teen. Vogue. I used to subscribe to all of them when I was in high school. I remember spending literally hours staring at those picture-perfect faces, hair styles, and very hip clothes.

I was into it.

I wanted to be like those models. You could find me in front of the bathroom mirror, trying out different poses. I was constantly trying the hot new way to line my eyes, roll my hair to get the right bounce, and enhance my skin with the latest mask. (That homemade oatmeal mask didn't work too well until I realized I was supposed to use the blender to make it into a *powder!*)

And clothes. Whatever the top models strutted down the

runway in, I wanted it. In fact, I bought those fashion extreme Vogue Patterns and actually *made* my own clothes. I dreaded the thought of being caught wearing the same outfit as the girl next to me in history or choir. I admit I often got carried away. (Sure glad I've changed since then.) One year I made head-wraps to match the very vogue outfits I whipped up on my sewing machine. They were hot! OK, I admit I looked more like a member of a strange cult than a model, but hey—it was in style!

I cared little about what others thought. I was engrossed in my appearance.

I was buying into the beauty buzz big time!

My physical appearance had all my attention!

It didn't matter that I didn't yet come close to resembling those cover girls. I was determined to keep on trying!

Why? Because images of physical perfection surrounded me, just like they surround you. It's easy to get sucked in and carried away! The beauty message is so appealing. It can make us long to be something we are not... and it sets us up for disillusionment with ourselves and with life in general.

Are You Ad-dicted to the Media?

Our world's crazy beauty standard makes it tough for some girls to deal with what they see in the mirror every morning.

And that is exactly what advertisers want!

Magazine publishers and cosmetic companies want to make you think that there really *are* girls and women who have flawless faces and incredibly proportioned bodies.

Why?

So you will buy their products!

It's beauty by association!

They want us to believe that if we use their products, we will look as unbelievable as the girl in the ad.

Is this true? Will I look like her if I use the product?

No! That picture is retouched. Even *she* doesn't look like that in person!

This is the way it works. We buy and use the product and still look the same as before. We get discouraged, but the company gets our money. Big bucks! That's the motivation behind it all! The beauty industry is a multi-billion dollar business.

GIRL TALK
Have You Ever Been Influenced by an Ad?

"Yes! One liquid powder foundation ad promised a natural, all-day foundation that would hide blemishes and reduce shine. My whole face was 'gunky' and felt slimy. It didn't help at all."   JodiLin, 16

"I bought a bottle of spray-on lightener to give my hair blonde highlights like the girl in the ad. Thanks to that I have *orange hair* in my tenth grade school pictures."
Kathy, 17

"I tried a new acne medication that promised clear skin in three days. Of course the model had clear skin, so I went for it. After the first night, my face was red and blotchy—making my acne even worse than before!"   Stephanie, 17

Challenge yourself to analyze ads. With the flawless models and the slick slogans, some of them are downright amusing!

A recent ad claimed that the most unforgettable women in the world wear a certain product. Well, you want to be unforgettable, don't you? No sweat. Just wear these products and no one will ever forget who you are! Yeah, right.

Another popular product pompously proclaims that if you weren't born with it (meaning some imaginary ideal of physical perfection), you can just use this product and people will think you were! Tee hee!

We need to beware of the media's power to cause us to feel discontentment with our God-given appearance. We need to put up our guard and be ready for their schemes!

Are *you* buying into the beauty message that bombards you from every angle? Take this quiz and find out if you need to be rescued!

BEAUTY QUIZ:
Are You Hip to the Media Hype?

1. Models obviously don't have moles, freckles, or birthmarks since you never see them on the cover girls.

    ___ TRUE   ___ FALSE

2. Models and actresses have small pores and flawless skin, and absolutely no pimples!

    ___ TRUE   ___ FALSE

3. If a company promises specific results when you use their product, they will deliver because the ad says so!

    ___ TRUE   ___ FALSE

4. Beautiful women are always nice, kind, and basically good people.

___ TRUE   ___ FALSE

5. Being pencil-thin comes naturally to models and actresses.

___ TRUE   ___ FALSE

6. Attractive women have easier lives; things just go their way.

___ TRUE   ___ FALSE

7. Most girls feel much better about their looks after reading fashion and beauty mags.

___ TRUE   ___ FALSE

8. Only women with large breasts appear on the *Cosmopolitan* cover or the Victoria's Secret catalog.

___ TRUE   ___ FALSE

9. Women who *look* beautiful *feel* beautiful.

___ TRUE   ___ FALSE

10. If you dish out ten dollars for mascara, it will work better than the $2.99 brand.

___ TRUE   ___ FALSE

CHECK YOUR ANSWERS!

1. False - Everyone has some body markings! You'll discover the illusion in a minute or two.

2. False - Many models have oily, large-pored skin that breaks out regularly. So, what's their secret? Dermatologists!

3. False - Lots of products make empty promises.

4. False - Our culture often confuses beauty with goodness. They aren't the same thing.

5. False - Few women are naturally thin. Due to the fact that the camera adds ten to fifteen pounds of "visual weight," models must force themselves to maintain an *unnatural* thinness, usually by maintaining unhealthy eating habits!

6. False - Only on the soap operas and in movies!

7. False - You knew this one was false! Teens tend to compare themselves to flawless faces on the magazine covers and feel discouraged as a result.

8. False - Stay tuned for the secret of small-breasted models!

9. False - Feeling beautiful is not based on appearance. It is based on a healthy self-esteem and close relationship with the Lord.

10. False - I've tested lots of mascaras, and it turns out that you don't always get what you pay for. Don't be fooled! More expensive does not automatically mean it is better!

Scoring

So, how did you do? If all of your answers are false, congrats! You aren't fooled by any beauty buzz.

If your answers were half true and half false, that's pretty normal! You're starting to clue-in to the media hype.

If all of your answers are true, you have been buying in to the beauty buzz big time! Beware, you have swallowed society's beauty messages hook, line, and sinker! This chapter is going to be an eye-opener for you!

An Inside Look at the World of Modeling

It took me a while to catch on, but I eventually did!

When I was nineteen I was on top of the world. I had just signed a contract with Wilhelmina Models, Inc. in New York City. I felt nearly invincible as I unpacked my bags to get settled in the Big Apple. The possibilities before me seemed endless. I quickly sought out a vocal instructor and the best acting coach around.

I felt like I was on my way!

The first few months were spent taking a million photographs. Close-ups, full-length, indoors, outdoors, glamorous evening wear, sporty tennis outfits! The agency and I worked to pull together my "look" and assemble a fabulous portfolio.

Finally I was ready to pound the pavement in search of work, pursuing my dream to be a model and actress. Day after day, I headed out to my *go-sees*—that's model talk for interview. I would "go to see" if I was the right person for the job.

I learned quite quickly that the modeling world is highly competitive, a cut-throat type of business. If a photographer or ad agent didn't like my look, they told me… right to my face! It was a brutal lesson for this Midwestern girl who had been raised to be kind and respectful.

Going from interview to interview I would usually be told why I was *not* right for the job.

Your *nose* is too short!

Your *eyes* are too round!

Your *hair* is too curly!

Your *lips* are too full!

You're not *tall* enough!

You're not *busty* enough!

All day long, day after day, I was constantly being criticized! How do you think I began to feel about myself?

Right! Like doo-doo!

And it wasn't just me! My roommates were going through the same thing. I *did* get some great print jobs and national commercials. I also appeared on the covers of several smaller magazines.

But, two years later when I left N.Y.C., I felt like my face was all wrong, my body was all wrong! Nothing about my physical appearance was acceptable!

My confidence slowly slipped away. When I looked in the mirror I no longer saw a God-designed young lady with bright eyes and a quick smile. Instead, I saw an ugly mole on my cheek. An absurd indent between my nostrils. Eyebrows that weren't perfectly arched. A thick waistline. Hips that were not rock-hard.

Why did this happen?

How did my view of myself get so distorted?

Here's how! I was being compared to our world's *unrealistic* beauty standard! A standard that is impossible to measure up to!

BEAUTY QUIZ:
Spot the Beautiful Babe "Must-Haves"

Exactly what does our society stamp its beauty approval on? I'll bet you can circle the right answer without giving it a second thought:

A	**or**	**B**
high cheekbones		flat cheekbones
crooked, yellow teeth		straight, white teeth
flawless skin		zits and moles
small, round eyes		almond-shaped eyes

A	**or**	**B**
full lips		thin lips
short eyelashes		long eyelashes
tall, thin body		short, heavy body
flab		muscles

CHECK YOUR ANSWERS!

A, B, A, B, A, B, A, B.

See! I knew you would get those! We all know what characteristics our world labels "must-haves" for beauty queens!

It hasn't always been this way. Society's definition of beauty has changed over the years. Long ago you were considered beautiful and prestigious if you were plump! Study the models used in paintings by the old masters. Exquisite facial features? No. Skinny, bony bodies? No. They were hefty and hearty looking. In those days, being "full-figured" was a sign of wealth. It was proof that you could afford the finest of foods in unlimited quantity. Big was beautiful.

Not so these days! Magazine covers, advertisements, billboards, and television have all pounded in the message that the beautiful face is flawless, the beautiful body is thin. Perfect face, perfect body.

Even those glamorous gals—the ones who make mega-bucks gracing the covers of the hottest magazines—struggle with their appearances!

One top model has said that women would be shocked if they really knew what she has to go through to maintain a lean body and a flawless face: starvation dieting, passing out at photo shoots, depending on dermatologists and plastic surgeons. A high price to pay for trying to live up to an impossible image of perfection.

If we idolize the flawless faces on magazine covers, believing that they project the true image of beauty, we are in *big, fat trouble*. We set ourselves up for *defeat!* The typical American female does *not* look like a cover girl!

The world's standard of physical perfection is unrealistic. It is unattainable, out of our grasp. It is absolutely, 100 percent impossible for one person to have *all* the characteristics our society dictates as necessary in order to be beautiful!

Unless, of course, your name is BARBIE!

You know—Barbie Doll!

She has no zits, moles, freckles, birthmarks, bruises, or blisters. No cellulite or stretch marks. No wrinkles or smile lines. Her curves are in all the right places. She has perfect lips, cheekbones, eyes, and straight, white teeth. Then, of course, there's her tight rear, long, thin legs and tiny feet, slender arms, and graceful hands.

Barbie has it all!

But Barbie is a doll. She's the plastic replica of physical perfection. If she were real, her measurements would be 36-18-33, and she'd have to be about eight feet tall!

We are NOT dolls. We do NOT have "Made by Mattel" stamped on our rears! Our stamp says "Made in Heaven"! We are one-of-a-kind designer originals (just a reminder in case you'd already forgotten!).

Yet, a lot of girls played with Barbie when they were younger and grew up thinking they would *look* like Barbie. Did it happen? Do girls grow up to look like B?

Nope.

The truth is that we are not dolls. We are not pretend people. We are real.

Now You See It, Now You Don't!

You see, real girls have pimples, crooked noses, big feet, stubby fingers, bony knees, flat chests, limp hair, and soft bodies!

Oh, yeah? Then why do the girls on the magazine covers and in the cosmetic ads look perfect? Why don't they have acne and bad hair days?

Glad you asked. (By the way, it takes *hours* and often several hair and makeup artists to create that "naturally beautiful" illusion!)

First let me ask *you* a question. If you *see* something with your eyes, does that mean it is *real*?

If you see David Copperfield put a woman in a box, saw it in half, then separate the box, does that mean the woman is in two pieces?

If you see the daylight overtake the night and you can't see the stars, does that mean they no longer exist?

Think it over.

Do you believe everything you see? I hope not! Instead, believe this:

> **Every picture perfect face you see in print has been retouched to make it appear flawless and acceptable by society's standards!**

Read that again.

It's true! What we see is not reality. It's fake. It's an illusion created with the help of a computer or a skilled airbrush artist.

Here's how they make ordinary look extraordinary:

First, a scanner is moved over the original photograph to recreate its image on the computer monitor (screen). Then the photo is pulled into a program such as Photoshop. The program breaks the picture down into little squares called pixels. Next an assortment of tools in the program are used to manipulate (or change) the photo. Pixel by pixel, absolutely anything on the original photo can be changed! When the "touch-up" is complete, the computer prints the new, retouched photo, creating an image that's ready to hit the press!

Imagine it! A simple computer program can do any of the following:

★ Even out skin tones.

★ Remove acne, freckles, or moles.

★ Soften wrinkles and smile lines.

★ Trim waistlines.

★ Reduce hip size.

★ Whiten teeth.

★ Change hair color.

★ Lengthen lashes.

★ Add or subtract blush color.

★ Use shading to create high cheekbones.

The possibilities are endless! I am convinced that even supermodels and actresses catch a glimpse of their perfected, retouched faces and think, *Gee, I wish I really did look like that!*

The July 1992 issue of *Cosmopolitan* is one of my all-time favorite magazine covers. It features Cindy Crawford posing in a gold-beaded bikini (as if you'd really wear *that* to the beach). She has one arm up with her hand behind her big, windblown hair. The other hand is on her hip.

It's an amazing thing to see. Cindy has perfectly even skin tones, no skin fold lines on her knuckles, and *no* underarm hair! No stubbles!

Is this reality? No way.

Oh, did I mention the fact that she is also *bursting* out of that teeny-weeny gold bikini top? Now girls, can we talk? Woman to woman? The straight scoop? Good.

The majority of the time, the perky, big breasts that you can't help but notice (and perhaps envy) are only about half real! Often the colossal cleavage you see is constructed—pixel by pixel—by adding various shades of brown in the perfect places, creating roundness and depth.

We're talkin' computer-created cleavage!

So don't believe everything you see!

Yes, a *few* models are well-endowed. Some naturally, some with the assistance of a plastic surgeon and a few thousand bucks! (More on this is a minute.) But it is *not* natural for the typical model—a 5'8"-6'3" tall woman with small-to-medium-sized bones—to have booming boobies!

I happen to know this firsthand.

So... Is It Wrong to Change the Way We Look?

Living in a critical and judgmental world that promotes an unrealistic beauty standard is too much for some people. I know teens who have had their noses bobbed, ears pinned, breasts enlarged, and moles removed. One girl even tried collagen injections to decrease the depth of her dimples!

Where do we draw the line?

Can surface changes create contentment?

Certainly, tinting your hair, adding acrylic nails, or wearing colored contacts can be harmless. With the right attitude, these changes can be fun! (Always check to be sure it's OK with Mom and Dad first, though.)

Some changes are even necessary. Wearing braces to correct an overbite or to even out crowded teeth are often a must for health reasons.

What about surgery?

Reconstructive surgery is sometimes required due to accidents or illnesses. It can help some people recapture their original, God-given design.

But more often than not, cosmetic surgery is performed to *re-design* a God-given feature. Elective surgery is based on personal preference. I believe a person needs to pray and do some real soul-searching before scheduling a purely cosmetic surgery. The possible side effects and risks associated with surgery should also be taken into consideration. Possibilities include anesthesia, infections, bruising, nerve damage, blood loss, and *pain!* (Just think of all the reports on the dangers of silicone breast implants. Due to the silicone sacs leaking into the body, women have been struck with serious diseases, even death!)

Is the perfect look really *to die* for?

Of course not! The good news is, there are lots of things you can do to make the most of the features God gave you... naturally! Go make yourself a big bowl of popcorn, then get cozy and let's talk about it!

GUY TALK
Hey Guys, Do You Think Girls Are Too Judgmental About Their Appearance?

"Yes, I think they spend way too much time in the bathroom checking out every little strand of hair and stuff like that."
Brad, 17

"Girls are very judgmental and tough on themselves. But I hate to hear them whine about their appearance. Actually, I probably don't notice half the things 'wrong' with them until they willingly point them out." Rusty, 17

"I hate to generalize, but for the most part, girls are just too hard on themselves. It's a real turn-off. Plus, it puts more pressure on guys to only date some cardboard cut-out."

Jordan, 16

"I think girls are judgmental and complain just to try to get us to refute their comments and compliment them."

Stan, 15

BEAUTY BONUS
Enhance the Beautiful in You

Who needs computer retouching and cosmetic surgery? Not *you!* Enhance your natural beauty with these easy-to-do techniques.

You shouldn't use makeup as a shield to hide behind or to alter your facial features. When you use tricks of the trade to create an illusion (like making your lips look fuller or your wide nose more narrow), you are only fooling yourself. Go with the features God gave you!

Here's how to make them shine.

Foundation sure beats big-buck airbrushing for evening out skin tones!

Color test the foundation on your jawline to ensure a perfect match. Using a cosmetic sponge or your fingertips, apply it evenly to your entire face, eyelids, and even your lips. Be sure to wipe it off your eyebrows, however. No need to put it on your neck, just blend at your jawline.

Polish off your look with powder!

This sets the foundation, soaks up excess shine, and helps powdered blush and eyeshadows glide on more smoothly! Select a loose or pressed powder and apply it with a big, fluffy brush. A colorless powder will do the trick unless you are skipping foundation and applying powder first. If so, choose a skin-toned powder instead.

Want to define your eyes and make your lashes look fuller?

Do it with **eyeliner**! Using a soft-kohl pencil or a regular shadow in a neutral tone like brown, brown-black, or soft charcoal, apply the liner directly against your lashes. (Blue, green, purple, and other bright colors detract from a natural look. Remember, you want others to notice *you,* not your makeup.) Guide the pencil along your top lashes, beginning at the outer corner of your eye. Three-quarters of the way in, blend the pencil line with your lashes so it's not obvious where the line ends. Never line on the inner lid next to your eyeball! Repeat under the lower lashes. Obviously, eyeliner is optional. You may want to save it for special occasions.

Hey, there, bright eyes!

You don't have to change the color of your baby blues to make them look their best! Try this **eyeshadow** idea. You warm skin-toned gals (whose skin tones are more golden or peachy beige than pink) look great in ivory, peach, brown, and mocha-toned shadows. Cool girls (whose skin tones are more bluish pink than beige) choose pinks, burgundies, mocha pinks, and

mauves. This same color rule also applies to your blush and lipstick colors! First, apply a light shade of shadow over your entire eyelid. Second, apply a medium-toned shadow three-quarters of the way across the lid, leaving the inner one-quarter showing the first color. Extend the shadow up into your crease. For extra depth, use a third tone on the outer one-quarter of the eye. Blend.

No falsies for you!

Make your *eyelashes* fabulously full with my (until now) *secret* technique! Use the top of your brown or brown-black **mascara** wand to coat just the *ends* of each lash (upper and lower). Give it a minute to dry. Now go back through your lashes, covering them with mascara from the root to the top this time. Be sure to work the wand into your lashes, twirling it as you coat the lashes. Tip your chin down, looking up into the mirror to apply mascara to your bottom lashes. Come up underneath them.

Face lifts are a total waste!

Enhance those cheekbones the natural way! The color of your **blush** will once again depend on your skin tones—warm or cool. Using your blush brush, apply light, even strokes, directly in the center of your cheekbone, starting next to your hairline and working toward your nose. As a general rule, blush should not be applied on your cheeks any lower than the bottom of your nose and no farther toward your nose than the center of your eye.

*Note: Light-skinned girls need a light-toned blush. Medium tones use medium. Dark skins look best in deep colors. The less contrast between your skin tone and your blush intensity, the better.

Collagen inserts in YOUR lips?

You've gotta be kidding! They are already "fearfully and won-derfully" made! Just add a light-colored, glossy **lipstick** to your lovely lips. Use your natural lip line as the guide. Now, let those pearly whites show through in a big, friendly smile and you're ready to go!

(Adapted from "The Beautiful You," *Brio* magazine, January 1992)

five

Live to Eat—or Eat to Live?
Healthy Eating Habits to Last a Lifetime

*O*ur culture idolizes the perfect body... perfect according to a ridiculous standard. We see thin, trim, lean-and-mean models and actresses all the time. The fat-free body is put up on a pedestal as a prized possession—something to be worshiped. Something to be achieved. A symbol of success. A mark of true worth... STOP!

The pressure for perfection has driven girls to take drastic measures, to declare war on their bodies. Attitudes toward food and fitness have gotten so off-track, girls frequently compromise their health without counting the cost!

It's time for a fresh perspective! I think it's time for a reality check! Let's get real!

The average fourteen-year-old girl of 5'3" weighs 110 pounds. By the age of eighteen, she is 5'4 1/2" and weighs about 128 pounds. Her taller friends will average from 130-180 pounds! That is reality!

It is estimated that the average American woman is 5'4" and weighs 146 pounds. Sixty percent of them wear a size twelve or larger, and about thirty-five million over a size sixteen. Not a size four! (Of course, being overweight is not healthy either. More on this coming up.)

A model's bod is a far cry from the typical female's. Models usually weigh 25 percent below average. That means they average 5'9" and 120 pounds! And it rarely comes naturally. They are forced to work out excessively and restrict their food intake to near-starvation levels. A few pieces of dry lettuce, a quarter breast of chicken, and a few crackers just won't cut it! The fear of losing jobs and the watchful eye of the media cause many models to abuse their bodies.

I know. I've been there.

Our society's phobia of fat has us craving thinness and clinging to the scale in hopes of reaching an "ideal" weight. (A note about weight charts: Charts cannot take bone structure, muscle mass, or metabolism into consideration. They are limiting. Ask any doctor: weight is a very individual matter, and therefore there *is* no such thing as an ideal weight.)

We compliment a friend's weight loss, praising her for her accomplishment. Is this right? Listen to the conversations you have with your friends. How often do your conversations center around eating, dieting, counting calories, avoiding fat grams, working out, or squeezing into your favorite jeans?

It's time to "STOP THE INSANITY" (to quote a famous fitness figure).

Caring for Your Body—God's Temple

Christ has called us to a better way of living! According to the world's standard? No way. To *God's* standards. Romans 12:2 (TLB) tells us this:

> Don't copy the behavior and customs of this world, but be a new and different person with a fresh newness in all you do and think. Then you

will learn from your own experience how his [God's] ways will really satisfy you.

God has a better way! He wants us to take care of our bodies. Why? Because they are the *home* of the Holy Spirit. That's right. When you have prayed and invited Jesus into your heart, God sends the Holy Spirit to live within you (check out John, chapter 14). Our bodies are his temple.

Haven't you yet learned that your body is the home of the Holy Spirit God gave you, and that he lives within you? Your own body does not belong to you. For God has bought you with a great price. So use every part of your body to give glory back to God.   1 CORINTHIANS 6:19-20 (TLB)

God wants us to keep our temples in tip-top shape, not so we look like supermodels or buffed-up babes, but so we can feel our best and be our best as we carry out the special assignments he has planned for each of us!

The key to your temple tune-up is sensible, balanced eating coupled with consistent, effective exercise.

Let's look at healthy eating first.

Eating Your Way to Health

What you choose to put in your body affects how good it looks *and* how well it operates. Just like gas is fuel to a car, food is fuel to your body. If you put water in your car, will it run? No. If you use regular gas when your car needs unleaded, will it run? Yes, but not very well. Now, if you fill your tank with super unleaded... your car will purr like a kitten!

It's the same way with your body. If you feed it junky, high-fat foods and lots of sodas and sugary treats, it will operate, but you will feel tired, sluggish, and depressed. Plus, you'll probably struggle with concentrating and getting things done.

Now, if you choose foods that are power-packed with vitamins, minerals, enzymes, amino acids, and all the healthy nutrients you need, you will feel good and perform at your peak. You will be motivated and alert. Just think, you can actually pay attention through Mr. Hicks' boring history lectures! You can find the energy to go to youth choir, even after a tough day at school. You might even be less apt to snap at your little sister for borrowing your new lip gloss!

See, when it comes to food, what matters most is not how *much* you eat, but *what* you eat. For instance, when you get home from school, totally starved, you can snack on an apple, a banana, and a handful of pretzels (that's a lot!). *Or* you can grab about a half a cup of peanuts (not much, huh?).

Here's the catch. This first snack has about 220 calories and less than 2 fat grams. The peanuts are packed with 450 calories and 35 fat grams. (The recommendation for teens is about 2,000 calories and 65 fat grams per day, but remember, every body is different.) With the fruit and pretzels you get more to munch on, plus the nutritional value is fabulous!

And more nutrition is exactly what teens need. Now is the time to set the stage for a healthy body, for today and the future! The typical teen diet is a nutritional nightmare. A bowl of sweetened cereal, a toasted pastry dripping with icing, powdered doughnuts, a burger and fries, Cokes, corn chips, candy bars, half a bag of cookies, a drive-through milkshake, a gooey sundae before bed... STOP! This all adds up to clogged arteries, sugar highs (and lows), and excess pounds. That's not the way to take care of God's temple!

Building a Better Bod with the Food Guide Pyramid

You can build a better body using the U.S.D.A.'s Food Guide Pyramid as your guideline. This will help you choose foods that are healthy. It will guide you in selecting a variety of foods so you get the vitamins, minerals, and nutrients your body needs. You'll be so energized—even your brain will feel a boost!

Remember, the Food Guide Pyramid isn't about crash dieting (fad diets are *never* the answer) or about developing an obsession with counting calories and figuring fat grams. That can drive a girl crazy! We're talking about an overall *lifestyle* adjustment—changing the way you think about food. THINK HEALTH! Yep, it's true that the pyramid will help you reduce calories and fat grams, since the foods that are most nutritious are naturally low in calories and fat, but health is your main focus.

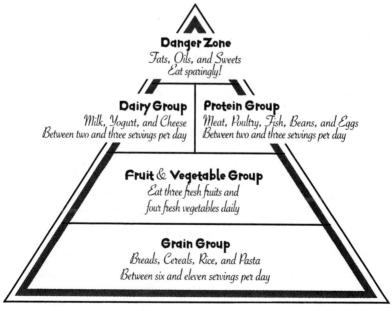

Danger Zone
Fats, Oils, and Sweets
Eat sparingly!

Dairy Group
Milk, Yogurt, and Cheese
Between two and three servings per day

Protein Group
Meat, Poultry, Fish, Beans, and Eggs
Between two and three servings per day

Fruit & Vegetable Group
Eat three fresh fruits and
four fresh vegetables daily

Grain Group
Breads, Cereals, Rice, and Pasta
Between six and eleven servings per day

First, take a look at the way the pyramid is divided up. The lower levels of the pyramid are bigger—that means you need to eat more of the foods from those groups. Likewise, you need to eat less of the foods that are higher on the pyramid.

The bottom level of the pyramid, the Grain Group, contains the foods that should provide the bulk of your diet. Help yourself to between six and eleven servings per day. This includes foods like **whole grain** breads, cereals, rice, and pasta. (Try multi-grain breads, oatmeal, brown rice, whole wheat, or buckwheat pasta.) One serving of this group is equal to 1 slice of bread, 1/2 cup of rice or pasta, or 1-4 ounces of dry cereal (depending on the density).

The second level is the fruit and vegetable food group. Eat three fresh fruits and four servings of raw veggies daily! A serving is equal to one piece of fruit, 3/4 cup juice, 1/2 cup cooked or canned fruits or vegetables, or 1 cup fresh fruit or raw vegetables.

It's best if you eat these raw, since these are LIVE foods, full of enzymes which are essential to good health! The nutritional value of food changes once it is cooked. Frozen is second best, and canned comes in last because many nutrients are lost in the canning process. If you do eat canned foods, choose fruits packed in water or unsweetened juices, and select veggies without salt.

These bottom two levels of the pyramid have you eating foods that are relatively low in fat, sugar, and calories and high in nutrients. They are also packed with fiber. Your body needs 25-35 grams of fiber per day. The average American gets 10-15 grams—not good! Fiber speeds up waste elimination, which reduces the potential for harmful bacteria escaping into your bloodstream. You can get a booklet that lists the fiber content in foods. (It includes fat grams and calories, too.) Educate yourself on what you let pass through your lips! Just to clue you in, 1 large pear has 6 grams of fiber. Four Twinkies have a big zero!

Breakfast cereals are a great way to get the bulk you need. One-third cup All-Bran has 8.5 grams of fiber. I usually mix my cereals; 1/3 cup All-Bran with something a little tastier like my homemade granola (stay tuned for my irresistible recipe).

OK, levels one and two are also your main source of carbohydrates, which your body needs for *true* energy! Sugar highs and caffeine rushes are NOT true, healthy sources of energy—no matter what the man at the cappuccino counter tells you.

As you move higher in the pyramid, the amount and size of servings become SMALLER! Level three introduces the dairy (milk) and protein (meat, poultry, fish, beans, eggs, and nuts) groups. Have two or three servings of milk, yogurt, or cheese per day. Select the low-fat, skim, or nonfat brands of each of these. One serving is equal to 1 cup milk, 8 ounces yogurt, or 2 ounces of cheese.

The protein group allows for two or three servings. Think about eating actual meat only once a day. And definitely limit red meat to once or twice a week. Skinless chicken, turkey, and fish are the best selections from this group. Baking, broiling, or grilling—without butter or sauces—is the healthiest. Other great sources of body-building protein are beans, peas, lentils, eggs, and nuts. A serving is equal to 3 ounces of meat, poultry, or fish, 1/2 cup beans, peas, or lentils, 1 egg, or 2 tablespoons peanut butter.

Look out for the Danger Zones! Climb on up to the top of the pyramid! This is the **danger zone**. Fats, oils, and sweets should be eaten sparingly.

Your body needs a certain amount of the "good" fats to

function properly. These fats are found in nutritious foods. It's the "bad" fats you need to watch out for!

You can have no more than two servings of fat per day, according to the Food Guide Pyramid. Servings from this food group are *very* small—1 teaspoon butter or oil, 2 teaspoons regular salad dressing or mayonnaise, 1 tablespoon cream cheese, or 2 tablespoons low cal/low fat dressing or sour cream. Or you can have 1/8 of an avocado or 5 olives. (Kiss that regular Saturday night pepperoni-and-olive pizza feast good-bye!) Treating yourself occasionally to a slice of pizza is fine, but an excess of "bad" fat puts your body at risk for heart disease and certain types of cancers. Go to your local library to get the scoop on good fats and bad fats to know that you are consuming the best foods possible.

Sugary items are tantalizing to our taste buds, but add up to nothing more than empty calories! The liver converts sugars to fat and the quick energy boost sugar gives is quickly followed by a crash. Plus, sugar causes tooth decay and many believe it weakens the immune system! So, are you ready? Here goes... limit cake, pies, cookies, brownies, candy bars, and ice cream treats to one serving per *week*. (Yes, you *can* do it!)

Now, don't be fooled by pink and blue packets! Artificial sweeteners are lower in calories, but have been linked to cancer, memory loss, and other side effects in clinical studies. So, skip 'em! Choose baked goods sweetened with fruit juices or more natural, slow-burning sugars that have a few nutrients such as pure maple syrup, honey, barley malt, molasses, or brown rice syrup! Check out the radically healthy recipes at the end of this chapter!

Cokes and coffees are part of the American way, but both are potential health hazards. Challenge yourself to make healthier choices by drinking fruit juices, herb teas, and tons of water! Your body needs 6-8 glasses of pure water per day. Squeeze in a few drops of *fresh* lemon for a vitamin C sensation! Your body will thank you!

(Adapted from "Shape Up for Summer," *Brio* magazine, June 1995)

Eat Healthy? But What Do I Do When...?

Now there will be times when making good food choices could be difficult. It's tough when you're out with friends or in the hot lunch line at school, or when someone else is doing the cooking. But there are ways to make better food choices, no matter where you are!

Tips for eating at home. Talk with your mom (or whoever does the cooking at your house) about the Food Guide Pyramid. Start helping your mom plan and cook the meals! (She'll probably be glad you've offered to help!) Figure out where each food is on the Food Guide Pyramid, so you can build the healthiest menus.

Goin' through the drive-through? Yikes! The fast-food frenzy! What's a girl to do? Healthy eating doesn't mean you have to stop eating at quick picks, especially if all your pals are headed there after the football game! Just make WISE CHOICES. (Note: The numbers in parentheses after each food list the calorie count and fat content for each serving.)

Instead of...	Try...
Burger King's Chicken Sandwich (710/43)	BK Broiler (550/29) or Broiled Chicken Salad (200/10!)

Instead of...

Taco Bell's Taco Salad (840/52)

McDonald's Bacon,
   Egg, and Cheese Biscuit (440/26)

Try...

Bean Burrito (380/12)

Apple muffin (300/3)

Salad bars like Wendy's or Shoney's offer a great way to build your own high-fiber, low-fat salad with lots of fresh, raw fruits and veggies! To get all the fast-food facts, pick up *Harriet Roth's Fat Counter* or *The T-Factor Fat Gram Counter,* available at your local bookstore.

No more hot lunch hassles! You can control your food choices within the confines of campus if you PACK YOUR LUNCH! I know the thought may give you the willies. It may sound so geeky! But, get over it! Bagging up a couple pieces of fruit, some pretzels, carrot sticks, and a nonfat yogurt beats downing a greasy burger or a gooey ice cream bar. Don't rely on the hot lunch line or vending machine cuisine. Besides, when your friends get on the better-bod bandwagon, you won't be brown-bagging it alone!

No time for breakfast? Don't you *dare* skip a meal! Your body is counting on you! Check out these powerful punches for nutrition on the run! Whip up a high-energy smoothie. Made from totally natural ingredients, these low-fat, vitamin-packed drinks can brighten the breakfast doldrums and are a great alternative to the chips-and-dip routine of after-school snacks.

All you need to create these delicious drinks is a blender, two servings of soft fresh fruit, 1-1/2 cups of your favorite juice, 1/2 cup of something dairy (nonfat milk, low-fat buttermilk, or yogurt) and a natural sweetener. Add a few ice cubes and whirl it all together until a rich, creamy texture develops. Pour it into a frosty mug, take a sip, and wait for a burst of yummy energy to hit! Want extra thickness? Add more fruit or decrease the juice. Too thick? Add juice. Try pineapple juice and papaya or mango, or grapefruit juice with orange and banana. The combinations are endless. Be creative! Make up your own vibrant variations!

Healthy Munchies!

Need a snack? Instead of reaching for high-fat nachos or potato chips, try one of these healthy munchies.

pretzel sticks	flavored rice cakes
nonfat frozen yogurt	baked potato with salsa or BBQ sauce
Nutri-Grain bars	Health Valley Energy bars
frozen fruit bars	fresh veggies with low-fat dressing

air-popped popcorn with butter-flavored or cheese-flavored sprinkle

juicy fresh fruit with a touch of honey and a sprinkle of wheat germ

BEAUTY BUSTER
Eating the Bad When You're Mad, Sad, or Glad!

Do you ever notice that there are times when you are especially prone to overeat, or to eat the wrong things? We all have times when we're tempted to indulge. Here are the stories of three teens... do any of them sound like you?

* * *

Jill's mom reminded her three times to make her bed and wash the last night's dinner dishes before leaving the house. But after fixing her hair and ironing her new shirt, Jill was running late. The honking horn from Anna's car only made the pressure worse. So out she dashed, her bedspread still sprawled on the floor and the dinner plates stacked in the sink, hardened with spaghetti. Hours later Jill returned home to an irritated mother who grounded her for two weeks. Jill was instantly ticked. She headed for the kitchen and made herself a King Kong-sized, hot-fudge sundae, trying to eat her anger away.

***

It was Saturday night, and Nan was home alone with a mint-green clay mask on her face. Who could've guessed her skin would have erupted with pimples last Thursday? So Nan was having a pity party and watching old movies while her friends were out having fun. Feeling very sad and lonely, she cried rivers of tears and ate loads of chips, buttered popcorn, and cheesy nachos, hoping to lift her spirits.

***

Erica had panicked big-time over her history exam. Trying to sort out and memorize the dates and places of historical events had taxed her brain. But the test hadn't seemed as hard as she'd expected. Scanning for her name on the bulletin board where grades were posted, Erica felt a knot of anticipation. Scholl, Smithers, Snead—there it was. Her eyes widened in disbelief; her heart jumped. A 92 percent! Time to celebrate! She headed toward the vending machine and treated herself to some big, soft, chocolate chip cookies. She stopped for gas on the way home and continued her rejoicing with a bag of

M&M's. At home she polished off two bagels loaded with cream cheese. Nothing like a good pigout to reward herself.

***

Jill was mad. Nan was sad. Erica was glad. But all three girls responded to their feelings with *food!* While food can provide a temporary satisfaction, it usually leads to tiredness, break-outs, and, eventually, excess weight gain.

Emotions are fickle things, especially for girls. But using food to deal with them is not your best bet. Before you get caught in this routine, check out these constructive ways to feed your emotions and work through your feelings.

When you're *mad*... Anger is often involuntary. Something happens, and before you know it, you're mad. But anger can be lethal if allowed to grow. So, nip it in the bud. How? By forgiving whomever you're angry at. Whether it's yourself, your parents, or your friend, LET IT GO! Holding a grudge is not an option. God says we are to be slow to anger and quick to forgive (even if we're not at fault). Is there anyone *you* need to forgive?

When you're *sad*... Having the blues is a normal part of the ups and downs of life. But *staying* down and depressed is not. Try TALK THERAPY! Find a mature Christian—someone you trust—and let it all out! No one to talk to? Then write it out! Start a journal. Make a habit of writing when things start piling up on the inside. And God is always there to listen. Is there anything *you* need to talk about?

When you're *glad*... When you're happy, treat yourself to the extra rewards that come from sharing your cheerfulness. Try writing to your grandparents or to friends and telling them your good news. Take your happy attitude to an elderly neighbor or a nursing home. You'll be doubly blessed when you spread some love and excitement their way. Use your joy to brighten someone else's world. Who could you share *your* good mood with today?

(Adapted from "Food: Avoiding the BAD when you're MAD, SAD, or GLAD!" *Brio* magazine, September 1995)

If you're having trouble controlling your eating habits, it might help to "buddy up" with one of your friends. That way you can encourage each other! Talking with a parent or adult Christian friend about your concerns can also help.

Sometimes in an effort to control their weight girls can develop serious eating problems that require professional help. We'll talk more about those in the next chapter.

Remember... God loves you just the way you are. And with his help, you can CHOOSE to take care of the beautiful temple he has entrusted to you!

One more thing... Eating healthy is only the first step on the road to healthy living. The second half of this "healthy pair" is exercise! We'll talk more about this in chapter six. But now, let's close this chapter with a few more yummy ideas for healthful eating.

More Great Recipes!

Remember:
C=cup
tsp=teaspoon
Tbls=tablespoon

Luscious Lemonade

2 C water
1/2 C pure honey
8 C water
1-1/2 C freshly squeezed lemon juice
1 lemon, thinly sliced

Combine 2 cups water and honey in saucepan over medium heat. Stir until honey dissolves. In pitcher mix together all ingredients. Stir, refrigerate for an hour or two; serve over ice cubes. (Add more honey for a sweeter taste!)

Watermelon Pops

Remove seeds from fresh watermelon. Blend in a food processor or blender, a few chunks at a time. Fill plastic popsicle molds or paper cups (add sticks after 1-1/2 hours). Freeze for 3-4 hours. Unmold and enjoy!

Great Granola

2 C oats
1 C chopped or slivered almonds
1/4 C pure maple syrup
1/4 C canola oil
2 tsp vanilla
1 tsp cinnamon
1/4 C wheat bran
Optional: Coconut, raw sunflower kernels, chopped dates, raisins. Add *after* baking!

Preheat oven to 325 degrees. Mix together all ingredients until well-coated. Spread on a large cookie sheet. Bake for 25 minutes, stirring once during baking time. Great as breakfast cereal, snack, or sprinkled on top of fresh fruit, yogurt, or frozen yogurt!

Carob-Oat Cookies

1/2 C butter
1/2 C plus 2 Tbls honey
1 egg, slightly beaten
1 tsp vanilla
2 C shredded coconut
2 C rolled oats
3 Tbls carob powder

Preheat oven to 350 degrees. Cream butter and honey together. Add egg and vanilla. Stir well. Mix coconut, oats, and carob powder in a separate bowl. Then add to mixture. Drop in tightly packed tablespoons onto a greased cookie sheet. Bake for 15-20 minutes. Don't overbake. Cool on cookie sheet.

Healthy Carrot-Date Muffins

1 C grated carrots
1/2 C whole wheat flour
1/2 C bran
2 tsp baking powder
1/4 tsp baking soda
1/2 tsp salt
2 Tbls vegetable oil
1/4 C molasses
1 egg
1/2 tsp vanilla
3/4 C apple juice
1/2 C chopped dates (or raisins)

Preheat oven to 375°. Mix together oil, molasses, egg, vanilla, and apple juice until smooth. Stir in bran and grated carrots. Let stand for 3 minutes. Combine remaining ingredients together, then add to bran mixture. Stir. Add juice if too dry. Fill greased muffin tins 3/4 full. Bake about 15-20 minutes.

six

The Perfect Look—Is It to Die For?
From Body Conscious to Health Conscious

*H*ealthy eating and exercise go hand-in-hand! Round out the new way you are caring for your body by adding a winning workout. In this chapter you're going to learn fun and healthy ways to get the exercise you need to look good and feel great. Then we're going to dive into the difference between body and health consciousness!

But first, get your fitness facts straight! Take this quiz, and see how you fare.

FITNESS QUIZ:
Fact or Fiction?
Check your answer!

1. Exercise has to be painful to be productive!
   ___ TRUE ___ FALSE

2. Naturally thin people really don't need to work out.
   ___ TRUE ___ FALSE

3. Regular exercise helps stamp out stress and banish the blues.
   ___ TRUE ___ FALSE

4. You can eat *anything* you want as long as you work out!

    ___ TRUE ___ FALSE

5. Following a long, hard workout, your body keeps on burning calories for hours.

    ___ TRUE ___ FALSE

6. Only aerobic exercise has lasting value.

    ___ TRUE ___ FALSE

7. If you exercise on a consistent basis you need to eat more, especially foods high in complex carbohydrates.

    ___ TRUE ___ FALSE

8. Exercising during your period can make cramps worse.

    ___ TRUE ___ FALSE

9. Physical activity builds a healthier bod *and* boosts your energy level.

    ___ TRUE ___ FALSE

10. It's a good idea to give yourself a full hour or more after you eat *before* you start your fitness fun.

    ___ TRUE ___ FALSE

Absolute Answers: 1. False; 2. False; 3. True; 4. False; 5. True; 6. False; 7. True; 8. False; 9. True; 10. True

Now that you've got a few fitness facts squared away, let's get started!

The Circuit Workout

One creative way to build your bod is through circuit training. The idea is to keep moving from one exercise to the next with little rest in between until you've completed all the exercises in the "circuit." No fancy health club needed! This fifteen-minute circuit training course can be done in the privacy of your own bedroom or backyard.

The big bonus with circuit training is that it increases cardiopulmonary fitness (yep, that's your heart and lungs) while toning muscles and increasing overall body strength. Plus, this routine combines both whole body (aerobic) and selected muscle group (anaerobic) exercises, ranging from low to high intensity, which is exactly what your body needs! It's a total-body workout!

Get Ready!

Your circuit workout begins with a warm-up, just to make sure your muscles are awake. The warm-up prepares your body for the more challenging exercises on the circuit. It raises your internal body temperature, which helps boost your performance and prevents injury. You'll cool down at the end, which will allow your heart to return to its regular pace and will help keep those quads and calves from cramping up on you!

Here's how to test your intensity:

If you're working so hard that you can't carry on a conversation, slow down! But if you haven't even broken a sweat or feel the least bit winded, work a little harder.

Hey, beginners! Keep an easy-does-it attitude and do the circuit for a week or two without the weights. Allow yourself time to become familiar with the routine and for your body to adjust to your new workout mode! Remember, it's always a good idea to check with your doctor before starting an exercise program.

Get Set!

Lace up a pair of exercise shoes that provide cushion and arch support. Grab a jump rope, a clock or timer, a set of one- or three-pound weights (beginners can use a can of soup in each hand), and some upbeat tunes like DC Talk or Margaret Becker! Now clear away last week's clothes, your book bag, and that half-eaten bag of pretzels off your bedroom floor, and get ready to circuit train!

Go!

Do the following for **one** minute each, with no rests in between! Keep moving!

1. Heel lifts

Lift your heels one at a time, keeping the balls of your feet on the floor. Swing your arms easily at your sides.

2. Side steps

Step right, then bring your feet together. Then step left and bring your feet together again. Get into a good rhythm, then raise your arms to shoulder level. When you step left, your arms go right. When you step right, your arms go left. Keep your breathing regular.

3. Walking in place

Walk in place at a moderate pace. With each step, press your palms toward the ceiling, then down. When you feel ready, hold a weight in each hand and press the weights toward the ceiling, then down.

4. March

To finish warming up your body, march around the room, keeping your knees high. Put your arms straight out in front of you, then bend at the elbow (a 90-degree angle). Pump your arms up and down out in front while you march.

5. Stretches

Spend thirty seconds on your upper body, then thirty seconds on your lower body. First, the upper body: Place your hands on your hips, feet shoulder width apart. Bend and stretch to the left, back, right, front.

For the lower body, do toe touches with a slight bend of the knees. Stretch toward the right foot, center, left foot, center.

6. Jumping jacks

Jump in place with your feet shoulder width apart and your hands meeting straight above your head. Return to starting position and repeat.

7. Lunges

Stand with your feet shoulder width apart. Lunge forward with one leg, bending it until your thigh is parallel to the floor. Keep your back and head as straight as possible. Return to starting position. Pause for a second between lunges to help maintain your balance.

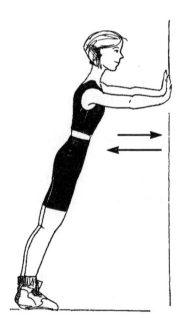

8. Push aways

Stand facing a wall with your feet 18-24 inches from it. Place your palms flat against the wall at shoulder height. Bend your elbows, dipping in; then push away from the wall.

9. Jump rope

Swing a rope, jumping with feet together or one foot at a time. If you're constantly getting tripped up, an imaginary rope will work just as well!

10. Curls

Stand with your back straight, your feet shoulder width apart. Grasp your weights (or cans) with your palms upward, arms at your sides. Bend your elbows, bringing the weights up toward your shoulders. Return to starting position.

11. Hopscotch

Imagine the squares right there in front of you! Hop down the squares, turn, and hop back.

12. Crunches

Hit the floor! Lie on your back with your knees bent, feet flat on the floor. Fold your hands behind your head. Lift your face toward the ceiling, hold, then back down. Don't do a full sit-up; these crunches are easier on your back.

13. Bicycle

Ready for a ride? Stay on your back and support your hips with your hands. Get those legs moving as if you were pedaling a bike.

14. Heel digs

Standing with your hands on your hips, touch your right heel to the floor directly in front of you. Now your left heel. Repeat.

15. Walking about

Simply walk around the room or in place for another two or three minutes, decreasing your pace as you go. Allow your heart rate to slow down. Follow with some slow stretches.

If you complete the circuit and still want more of a workout, take it again from the top! Or get creative and design your own outdoor circuit. Just so you don't get bored, alternate circuit training with another aerobic activity like walking, rollerblading, jogging, biking, or swimming. Start with fifteen minutes, working up to thirty or more. You can do it!

(Adapted from "Winter Workout," *Brio* magazine, February 1996)

Eating Disorders: When Body-Consciousness Turns Harmful

Sarah looked like your typical girl-next-door. But inside, her fears were raging. See, when Sarah's hormones kicked in at puberty, her hips, thighs, and bust areas filled out and took on a new softness. She panicked over the changes, concluding she was fat. To her, fat meant failure.

Sarah began downing diet pills and bingeing—eating lots of food, then throwing up. She dropped out of band and spent all her time working out! In a short period of time Sarah was a full-fledged bulimic and became very sick. Her parents put her in a hospital for treatment. There she learned about proper nutrition and how to care for her 5'1" large-boned body that would never be 5'9" and tiny!

Actress Tracey Gold understands those feelings and fears. Most recognized for her role as Carol Seaver in the ABC sitcom *Growing Pains*, Tracey has been very open about her struggle with anorexia (an addiction to dieting that results in self-starvation). She was forced to leave the show in order to fight for her life. She craved thinness. At an all-time low of eighty pounds and with the threat of death at her doorstep, she finally scared herself into reality. Thankfully, she realized that the perfect look was definitely NOT to die for! She now understands that her weight is not a reflection of her character. After much professional help, her weight has stabilized. But she could tell you that the roller coaster ride through an eating disorder is a nightmare.

Sarah agrees. "I hope others never go through what I've been through. Being afraid of food and hating your body is awful—you feel trapped, like there is no way out! But there is! I could not have made it through this without God's help!"

Sarah and Tracey. Two intelligent, warm, and talented young women. Both of them bought in to society's perfect body lie and fell prey to an eating disorder. An estimated eight million Americans are currently afflicted by these abnormal eating patterns, with thousands *losing* their lives as a result each year.

* * *

True eating disorders are way beyond typical dieting. Here are a few of the most common types of eating disorders:

Anorexia Nervosa

Anorexia is addictive dieting. It is a form of self-induced starvation. Anorexics have a compulsive need for perfection and control that is usually brought on by trauma. They risk their overall health, and can suffer from loss of menstruation, irregular heartbeat, heart attack, or heart failure. Other internal organs can suffer extreme damage as well. An estimated ten to fifteen percent of anorexics die, exchanging their lives for the need to be thin.

Bulimia Nervosa

This is when a person develops intense, secretive patterns of eating large quantities of food, known as binge-eating. This is followed by an intense and compulsive effort to get rid of the food and the "full" feeling by some form of purging (vomiting, excessive exercise, or using laxatives or diuretics). Bulimia can lead to dangerous weight loss, kidney failure, menstrual irregularity, swollen neck glands, muscle cramps, heart complications, and internal bleeding from the tearing of the throat lining (due to excessive vomiting).

Compulsive Eating

This is when a person consumes large quantities of food, without being able to control the amount she eats. (Relax, this is more than the occasional pigout.) The person feels compelled to eat. This is usually done to escape or numb out feelings that she is not dealing with in a healthy manner. Food alone becomes her comfort and her friend. Compulsive eaters gain unhealthy amounts of weight that can lead to obesity and health complications.

This is serious stuff! Crash diets, yo-yo dieting, and fad diets can mess up your metabolism and your menstrual cycle, and you should never abuse your body this way. But eating disorders mess up your *life!*

It's true that most teens do not develop a severe, full-blown eating disorder, but thousands of you teens out there are bowing to society's pressure to be thin. An obsession with being skinny can lead to twisted thinking about food, the body, and one's personal value. This can prompt girls to "dabble" in the dangerous tactics that are commonly connected to eating disorders.

What is your food bent? Would you call it healthy or unhealthy? Take this quiz to find out!

QUIZ:
How Healthy Is Your Attitude Toward Food?

1. Are your thoughts filled with food? Do you frequently find yourself planning your next pigout?

   ___ YES   ___ NO   ___ OCCASIONALLY

2. Do you read labels to figure out fat grams before you'll pop something into your mouth?

   ___ YES   ___ NO   ___ OCCASIONALLY

3. Are you self-conscious all day if your denims are hard to zip in the morning?

   ___ YES   ___ NO   ___ OCCASIONALLY

4. Do you plan your activities around food?

   ___ YES   ___ NO   ___ OCCASIONALLY

5. Do you *always* count calories on your mental calculator?

    ___ YES   ___ NO

6. If you don't get asked to the prom, do you automatically think it has to do with that five pounds you gained over spring break?

    ___ YES   ___ NO   ___ OCCASIONALLY

7. Ever notice what other people are chowin' down on and feel judgmental or envious of them?

    ___ YES   ___ NO   ___ OCCASIONALLY

8. Does your mood take a nose dive if the scale has gone up or if you've eaten too much?

    ___ YES   ___ NO   ___ OCCASIONALLY

9. Do you notice the models on magazine covers, in ads, or on television and think their bodies are the norm?

    ___ YES   ___ NO   ___ OCCASIONALLY

10. If you miss your workout two days in a row, does it make you feel like a fat failure?

    ___ YES   ___ NO   ___ OCCASIONALLY

11. Are you pumped when you've had enough willpower to skip meals?

    ___ YES   ___ NO   ___ OCCASIONALLY

12. Ever pat yourself on the back when you feel thin, but put yourself down when you feel pudgy?

    ___ YES   ___ NO   ___ OCCASIONALLY

13. Do you ever hide food and eat it when no one is watching?

    ___ YES   ___ NO   ___ OCCASIONALLY

14. Have you ever turned to laxatives, antacids, or excessive exercise to get rid of that "full" feeling?

    ___ YES   ___ NO   ___ OCCASIONALLY

Scoring

How many times did you answer Yes? No? Occasionally? Count the number of each.

If your *nos* stacked up the highest, you have been able to take the perfect-body pressure in stride! Your approach to nutrition and exercise is healthy! Keep it up!

If you hung out in the *occasionally* column the most, keep an eye on your attitudes. You're being negatively influenced, but not to extremes. Take time to give a second look to the areas you are most hung up on!

For those of you who answered *yes* to six or more, we need to talk! Your unhealthy attitudes could have you headed straight toward an eating disorder. Don't let it happen! This chapter is vitally important for you!

The Danger Zone

Think about it.

★ Have you ever heard the girl in the stall next to you throwing up at school or at a party?

★ Are you aware of girls who are *always* running to the bathroom?

★ Do you know girls who carry laxatives in their purses?

★ Do you know of girls who skip breakfast and lunch, but drink coffee or sugary caffeinated colas all day to try to stay alert?

★ Have you met girls who compulsively smoke or chew gum to keep themselves from eating?

★ Do you know girls who take diuretics (water pills) to force their body to secrete larger amounts of urine in hopes of dropping a pound or two?

If you or a friend are playing in the danger zone, thinking you'll drop a few harmless pounds, it's time to sound an alarm! Experimenting with vomiting, laxatives, diuretics, compulsive exercise, and drastic dieting can be life-threatening. Pardon me for getting technical for a moment, but we need to scope out this scoop:

The Dangers of Vomiting

Did you know that stomach acid is strong enough to eat the skin and remove teeth enamel? Consistent vomiting forces stomach acid into the esophagus (throat), causing pain, swelling, tearing, and scar tissue—ugh—making it hard to swallow!

The Dangers of Diuretics

Diuretics, more commonly known as "water pills," cause the kidneys to pump out larger than normal amounts of urine, forcing out needed fluids. This, in turn, causes dehydration and electrolyte imbalance which can cause heart failure.

The Dangers of Laxatives

Laxatives are those tiny tablets that cause major bowel movements, diarrhea, water loss, dehydration, and constipation (if the body becomes addicted to them). Laxatives totally disrupt the body, affecting one's normal electrical circuit. This puts the respiratory system and the heart at risk. And hey, the gas pains and abdominal cramps are no picnic either!

The Dangers of Compulsive Exercise

When a girl insists on attempting to burn off every calorie she consumes or willingly puts her entire life on hold until her workout is complete, she's suffering from compulsive exercise. Exhaustion, overworked muscles, and an inability to maintain a healthy weight may result.

The Dangers of Drastic Dieting

Dressing for prom night, an important date, weighing-in for gym and the like often influence teens to turn to drastic dieting tactics. Is it OK to starve oneself for a short period of time? Perhaps the mega-headaches, fainting spells, and easily caught cold or flu that result will clue you in.

God has designed the body to work according to a delicate balance. Vomiting, diuretics, laxatives, compulsive exercise, and drastic dieting all mess up this balance, putting the body at risk.

How can you tell if you are in this "danger zone"? If you have concerns, it is best to talk with your doctor. However, many girls with eating disorders don't always see the problem until it has created *permanent* health problems. If you—or someone you know—is exhibiting two or more of the following signs, it's time for you to *get help!*

HELP FOR EATING DISORDERS

- Confide in your parents, a trusted adult, or your pastor.

- Contact RAPHA (Christian health care organization) at 8876 Gulf Freeway, Suite 340, Houston, TX 77017 or call 1-800-383-4673 and ask to speak to a counselor.

Ending the Search for Thinness

What causes a girl to mess around with harmful tactics that could in fact lead to a full-blown eating illness? Pressure, pressure, PRESSURE! From society, friends, family, peers—even internal pressure! Are the things we are being pressured to believe really true?

Let's examine some popular myths!

The Together Girl Is Good at Everything She Tries

Some girls believe the inability to be good at everything makes you a total failure.

WRONG! It is impossible to be good at everything. God has gifted each of us in the areas *he* has chosen. Those are the areas we need to develop and use to glorify him! So whether it's academics, sports, art, music, drama, auto mechanics, cooking, working with kids or the elderly, use your God-given ability to do your best and have fun while you're at it!

Physical Perfection Determines Your Value

By now you know all about this one. We don't have to live up to the world's beauty guidelines. *Your worth as a person is NOT based on your weight, shape, or size.* Better read that last sentence again! It is vital that you understand this. Only in God's eyes is there perfection. He already sees you as perfect—an exquisite work of art.

Having a Boyfriend Proves You Are Lovable

Girls are always falling for this one! Do you have to have a steady boyfriend—or a string of boyfriends—to prove you are truly desirable and lovable? Less than 50 percent of girls even date before college!

Listen up. Boyfriends may (or may not) come and go. Your security needs to be in yourself and your Lord. Jesus' sacrifice of love is the ultimate proof that you are worth loving (more on this great news coming up).

Still not convinced? Here's a word from the 1996 *Brio* Girl, Stephanie Cherry!

Up Close and Personal
with 1996 Brio Girl
Stephanie Cherry

"I've learned some important lessons from God about dating and feeling secure in who I am, with or without a boyfriend. God has created each of us as individuals, and whether you and I have a boyfriend or not, we are unique parts of his plan. That's pretty incredible.

"I've also learned that being picky isn't bad. I know so many people who have been hurt because they *weren't* selective about whom they dated. And for many of us, having a boyfriend is so important that we change who we are and what we stand for—just to attract them! Guys should accept us for who we are, treating us like princesses, and we shouldn't settle for anything less.

"Each night, I ask God to shape my life and that of my future husband. I pray that I would learn to be more like Jesus, and that someday I will be a pleasing wife. I must allow God to take the reins of my life in every area, including my dating."

(Adapted from "Stephanie Says," *Brio* magazine, February 1996)

Measuring Up Is a Must!

Using this world as a measuring stick can create feelings of inadequacy that can crack a girl's self-esteem, leaving her believing she is unacceptable. These feelings can lead to self-punishing behaviors. Why not do *the opposite?* God's measuring stick is what matters. He's not concerned that you have the coolest clothes, the latest curfew, or the curviest bod! He cares that you've been loving to your family, kind to your classmates, patient with your teammates, and at peace with life, trusting him in all things! Besides, 2 Corinthians tells us that as Christians our adequacy is from GOD!

The Picture-Perfect Life Really Exists!

Ever feel the pressure to appear as if everything in your life is neat and tidy? No problems. No ripples. No stress. No conflict.

We're talking here about putting up a front. But pretending life is perfect takes a lot of energy and keeps you from being yourself. Life gets crazy for everybody! If life was going to be pain-free and smooth sailing, God would never have had to send us the Holy Spirit! Remember, he's the Comforter! Obviously, we were going to need a little T.L.C.! So, drop the facade. In Christ, you are free to be real!

Now that you're clued in to the truths behind these myths, don't allow the pressure to get to you! You are unique and special just as you are! You're taking care of yourself through healthy eating and regular exercise. Are there other ways to care for the positively awesome you? You bet! On to chapter seven!

seven

Respect, with a Capital R!

Caring for Yourself in a Christ-like Way

*T*he beauty issue is settled! God thinks you're positively awesome—made in his image—hand-crafted according to his purpose! He has given you an awesome body with a look and bone structure unique to you and you alone! Your body is so precious to him he honors it by making it the home of his Holy Spirit (once you receive Christ into your life). He calls it a temple—a place of pure and holy worship unto him.

WHOA!

Ever thought of your body as a place of pure and holy worship to the Lord? What? It rarely crosses your mind?

Join the club!

Most of us forget the reverence and respect God has for these bodies that he so "fearfully and wonderfully" created! We often do things that trash our temples, making it tougher for the Holy Spirit to transform us into the image of Christ and to use us for God's glory. Eek!

I'll bet God would agree: it's time to stop trampling our temples and start to develop some balanced attitudes toward our bods!

This awesome bundle of flesh and bone really does deserve our respect. When we respect our bodies, we are honoring God! He's the one who gave our bodies to us as a *gift!*

A gift!

A gift to be respected! When you respect something you take special care of it. You pay particular attention to its needs, protecting it from anything that might be harmful.

Therefore, the level of respect we have for our bodies will be evident by the way we treat them! Do we care for our bodies' needs and guard them from danger? Our respect level will also cue God in on exactly how grateful we are (or are *not*) for his gift.

Gulp.

Let's brainstorm through a few ways we can show we respect to our bodies—and our God!

A Lively Lifestyle

By now you've got a great jump-start on caring for your bod by eating the right foods! I can see you now, nibbling on a carrot stick, chompin' on an apple, and gulping a glass of water! I can even hear your heart poundin'—a sure sign that your workouts are working!! So, keep it up—march, two, three, four!

Let's take all this one extra step. Get up off the couch and live! An active, lively lifestyle beats bedroom boredom any day! And it's better for your body!

Here are some pep-steppin' ideas:

★ Next time you're cruisin' the mall, scopin' out the sights, do your body a favor—take the stairs! Don't give in to the comfort and ease of the escalator or elevator!

★ Not *required* to take P.E. at school? Then *elect* to take it! Working in some physical activity in the midst of sitting on your seat all day, day after day, shows you care about your condition. It will also re-energize you—and help you stay tuned-in the rest of the day.

★ Stop circling the parking lot for that perfect spot! Pull into a place that makes you stride toward the store instead of merely strolling to the door!

★ After dinner, why shut yourself up in your stuffy bedroom? Go for a walk with a family member or friend. Use each step as an opportunity to catch up on their lives and share what's happening in yours.

★ Extra time on your hands? Invest it in those you love and those who love you! Especially those little people called younger siblings! Go outside for some Hide 'n Seek, London Bridge, Duck-Duck Goose, or Red Rover! Or use your imagination to organize some relays! Hope you don't think you are too cool to cut-up with the kids. Playtime is a great time to be active *and* to earn the respect of your brothers and sisters, nieces and nephews, and cute little cousins!

★ Before you flop down in front of the TV, do some bends and stretches by picking up clutter and putting it away—your bedroom mess included!

★ There's always the option of dragging your dad out to the "driveway court" for a little b-ball! Go ahead, shoot some hoops. It's guaranteed to build your bod and your relationship with the big guy!

An active life and an active attitude will help prove your respect for your body and keep it in tip-top shape!

Good Grooming

The secret's out! You can blast away bad breath, body odors, bad hair days, and nasty nails with good grooming. Show that you value yourself by taking good care of *you*—head to toe!

Body Basics

A clean, odor-free body with brushed teeth and fresh breath are sure signs of self-respect! Check out these timely tips!

★ Flash a confident smile with sparkling teeth and fresh breath by brushing several times a day! Using medium-soft bristles, brush in small, circular motions. Give an extra stroke on those hard-to-reach back teeth. Don't forget your tongue! It needs a once-over, too.

Toothpaste can do *more* than just taste good! Choose one with tartar control, fluoride, and baking soda. You can fight bacteria, plaque, and stains all at once! Speaking of stains, stay away from colas, coffee, and tea. For extra plaque-fighting power, be sure to floss regularly.

About that breath—don't stand for morning mouth or dragon breath. Use an effective mouthwash as part of your daily routine. Keep a travel-sized breath freshener spray closeby in your purse or book bag. When in doubt, pull it out!

★ Body odor kicks in when perspiration mixes with bacteria on your skin. Here's how to battle B.O.!

Daily showers using an anti-bacterial soap will help to eliminate odor! Pay special attention to those extra-odorous areas such as your "private parts." After you're dry, lightly powder the area with talc. Keeping clean is especially important during your period. Frequent changing of sanitary pads will help!

★ Lock in your underarm security and guard against wetness and odor! Odor-fighting deodorants and wetness-fighting anti-perspirants are available separately or together. Which is for you? It depends on your individual body chemistry, amount of perspiration and degree of underarm odor!

If any product causes a rash or itching, stop using it. Try another one. To avoid a shocking sting, wait ten minutes before applying protection to freshly shaven underarms!

(Adapted from "Delicate Details," *Brio* magazine, April 1994)

Hair Happenings

Maintain a squeaky clean mane and tame those tresses with these hair hints!

★ Shampoo, shampoo, shampoo! The first and most vital step in caring for your hair! Choose a pH-balanced product that matches your hair type (dry, normal, or oily) and texture (fine, medium, or coarse). Rub a quarter-sized dollop of shampoo between your palms. Then apply it evenly to your wet hair. Work the shampoo all the way to the roots, giving an extra scrub at your hairline and the nape of your neck.

★ Avoid a too-soft, too-tame, too-greasy look by applying only a tad of conditioner to the ends of your hair. This will help with tangles, too. Be sure to rinse both shampoo and conditioner thoroughly.

★ Keep your hair trimmed (every six to eight weeks) to maintain your hairstyle and avoid split ends. What causes them, anyway? The outer layer of the hair strand is worn away by hot rollers, curling irons, blow dryers, and the like, and what you get is split ends! Over-processing hair with perms and highlights doesn't help, either. Over-processing steals the natural bounce and shine from healthy hair!

★ Looking for a style that gives *you* style? Identify the look that's best for you by asking yourself these questions:
1. Is my hair type capable of achieving the style I want?
2. Does this style match my personality (bubbly, sophisticated, or sporty)?
3. Does my lifestyle lend itself to a quick style or a more decorative 'do?
4. Is this style suitable to my wardrobe (classic, contemporary, or trendy)?
5. Is this hairstyle in proportion to my height and weight?

Now check out your face shape! Steer clear of repeating your face shape with your hairstyle. If you have a **round** full face, stay away from a super curly and short style. Try a longer, straighter look. **Square** faces—keep your curls or fullness away from the corners of your forehead and jawline. **Oblong**? No prob! Wear your fullness at the cheekbone. **Pear-shaped**? Go for wavy or curls on your forehead and smoothness at your jawline. **Heart-shaped**? Save your fullness for your chin area! Balance is the key!

Well-cared-for hair says you respect yourself enough to take the time to look your best!

Manicure Magic

Put the final touch on your "I care" campaign with these ten tips for well-managed nails!

1. Remove old polish.
2. File down and shape nails into nice oval shapes using an emery board.
3. Soak tips of your fingers in warm, sudsy water for three to four minutes to soften the cuticles. Then push them back with a cuticle stick.
4. Clip away any loose skin.
5. Buff weak, thin nails with a buffer and vitamin-enriched cream. Scrub and rinse.
6. Seal dry nails using a clear base coat.
7. Apply two coats of professional nail polish. Allow drying time of fifteen minutes between coats. Choose light shades, avoiding unnatural colors like black, purple, blue, and orange!
8. Clean up polish smudges on skin with a remover-soaked cotton swab.
9. Apply clear top coat for long lasting luster!
10. For the pro-look, finish your manicure with a touch of nail oil. Rub along cuticle area.

What Do Your Clothes Say About You?

With today's crazy fashions and absurd attire, you have the opportunity to show you value yourself and honor the Lord by what you choose to wear!

Like it or not, fair or not, clothes talk! The way you dress sends a message to others! What are you communicating? Reverence? Rebellion? Respect? While the grunge look is comfy—droopy denims and all—it tends to look like the person wearing it is down on herself and life in general! Those mini-skirts, tight tops, midriffs, and plunging necklines have a little something to say, too!

Here's the point.

Dressing your best is far more than wearing the latest fads that plaster the pages of the magazines or copying funky store mannequins! Dressing with respect means dressing modestly. It means not conforming to any style that screams for the attention of others, turns heads in a tempting way, or communicates anything less than a heart that loves the Lord!

Same goes for your accessories, especially jewelry! Lots of today's necklaces, earrings, and bracelets are actually decorative designs and symbols that make statements you might not even be aware of! Six-sided crystals, zodiac signs, the yin-yang symbol, mood rings, eyeballs, bird feet with claws, skeletons, and snakes are all linked to New Age or occult beliefs. They may seem harmless, but they are tied in with powerful practices. In refusing to wear these symbols you give honor to the One *you* serve. If you're into symbols, wear the ones on "our side"! Crosses, angels, a fish symbol, or a True Love Waits ring all depict Christianity!

Secrets to Flatter Your Figure

Now while some clothes and accessories are just not appropriate, some are simply not appealing! Yep. It is more important to wear what looks *good* on you than it is to be decked out in a fashionable fad!

Why let designers dictate your look? You are an individual! Let your clothes be an outer reflection of your inner self. Unique! Creative! One-of-a-kind! That's a true fashion statement!

Here's a few secrets to styles that will flatter your figure in the finest way!

★ Small shoulders with full hips? Wear light colors on top with shoulder pads, pockets, and fullness to balance your pear shape.

★ Broad shoulders with slender hips? Wear loose fitting items with fullness on the bottom, keeping your shirts, tees, and blouses simple.

★ Super short? Try wearing the same color clothes from head to toe. It gives the illusion of height!

★ Tower tall? Steer clear of crop tops, short skirts, and mega-heels.

★ Balance your bod! Vertical lines add visual height. Horizontal lines create width. Diagonal lines add interest. Asymmetrical lines offset unevenness. Multi-stripes add bulk. Curved lines add softness. Utilize these illusions as needed!

GUY TALK
How Can You Tell if a Girl Respects Herself?

"When she cares for her appearance without overdoing it. Sort of simple but nice."   Dave, 14

"When she's secure enough to dress her own way—not weird, but naturally attractive."   Joey, 15

"A girl who respects herself will respect others and treat them like they matter!"   Mike, 15

"I can tell she values and respects herself if she can look me in the eye when we're talking. Confidence is appealing to me."
                                                        Nick, 16

"A girl respects herself when she doesn't do far-fetched stuff like triple-pierce her ears, get a nose ring, wear black nail polish and do-rags. That stuff looks like she doesn't even like herself."   Cliff, 17

Choose to Be Drug-Free!

This Bud's For You... **NOT**. Alcohol, drugs, and nicotine are all abusive substances to your body! They are definite temple-trashers.

Using these drugs is like pouring poison into your system. You probably know that drug use wreaks havoc on your body. Not only do drugs like alcohol and marijuana alter your sense of reason, your mood, your coordination, and your visual perception, they dilate your pupils, cause hallucinations, and kill irreplaceable brain cells. Drugs and cigarette smoking can damage nasal passages and sinus cavities and prematurely dry and age the skin. Drug and alcohol abuse is known to overwork the liver, kidneys, and heart. Using any of these drugs can result in serious diseases, even death. And of course drug use can seriously mess up a person's goals and destroy personal relationships!

So why do just as many Christian teens as non-Christian get wrapped up in the temporary high of these abusive substances? Good question. I bet God is wondering the same thing! After all, God has given us Jesus to satisfy our every need.

Need joy? An escape from the pressures of the world? A sense of peace? Answers to problems? Feel the need to fit in somewhere? A place to belong?

Drugs are not the solution. You can find just what you need in Jesus. As you grow closer to him, you will honor God—and take better care of yourself—by saying, "The choice for me is drug-free"!

Up Close and Personal
with "Jayme Wess"

Have you ever thought that because you are a Christian you will never be tempted to do "really bad" things? This is about a girl who discovered that even Christians can make wrong choices and be trapped by evil. The good news is God's love prevails when we turn back to him! Her name has been changed to protect her privacy, but her story is real.

"I started drinking, doing drugs, and smoking in eighth grade after I switched from a private Christian school to public school. I was just drawn to the 'bad' kids. I've always been a thrill seeker, and my new friends provided some new ways to sneak around and have fun! I started doing it for kicks, but soon I found comfort in the way it made me feel. It gave me a sense of belonging, dulled reality, and suffocated any guilt.

"I came from a Christian family and didn't have any real problems. But I decided that I was young and would put Christianity on a shelf. I figured I'd do the Christian thing when I grew up. I hardened my heart so that what I did wouldn't matter. Meanwhile I wanted to live it up.

"By the end of eighth grade I had earned myself quite a reputation. My wildness had gotten so out of hand I nearly killed myself. I almost died behind a movie theater due to alcohol poisoning. The incident only slowed me down for about five months, then things picked up once again in high school.

"Things just seemed to snowball to where I couldn't get out because I was in so deep. I was dependent. As things progressed into harder drugs, bars, and guys, I thought it was just too late. I knew what was right, but I wasn't strong enough to do it.

"I had *no* respect for myself, therefore, I became my own worst enemy. I hated who I had become and couldn't get away from me! It's impossible to run away from yourself!

"I didn't care if I ruined my body. I didn't like it anyway. I was already angry at God for not giving me the slender kind of body I wanted. I didn't care for his 'gift' so I didn't care if his 'temple' got destroyed.

"Ironically though, I did play sports throughout all these party years. I was into tennis, but it became a joke that I had won more matches hung over than I had sober. I also played soccer. During a game late in the season, I got hit and broke my nose because I had been 'tripping hard' on acid the night before.

"Needless to say, things had gotten out of hand. My parents tried to help, but I saw their caring attitudes as attempts to be controlling and I resented that.

"But thankfully, when I started college, God got ahold of my heart and wouldn't let go. I prayed that he would take me back and help me get off the fence I was teetering back and forth on.

"It was tough. With God's help I started changing many of my circumstances. I had to let go of old friends and find new forms of entertainment—no more going to bars. I admit that my will was pitted against God's will. I knew the final choice was up to me. But I found that the more you say no to something, the easier it gets and pretty soon you start feeling better about yourself.

"My life which had been in shambles slowly started to take shape. I had stayed in church during this time and finally got into a Bible study. Then a brave youth pastor saw God's potential in me and asked me to help with the girls' program.

"The accountability and the encouragement of my 'boss' really helped me get off the fence and be committed to following God.

"The struggles are not over. Satan constantly tries to invade and tempt! But I know I'm on the right road. I have gained a new sense of confidence and respect myself much more than I used to.

> "My advice to teen girls? Pray hard, stay in God's Word, get a support team that believes in you, stay tight with Christian friends who are on the same road you are. And remember, every situation presents you with two choices—God's way or Satan's way. Choose God's!"

Value Virginity!

In a world that promotes and applauds teen sex, virgins stand out, sometimes whether they want to or not! Abstinence is one of the ultimate ways to show God you respect the gift of your body! Check out what these celebs have to say on the subject!

Celebrities Talk... on Sex

"I chose to remain a virgin until I was married, and I'm really glad I did."   Amy Grant

"Until you get married, run away from temptations as if Freddy Krueger is two steps behind you. Abstinence can save your life."   Dave Dravecky, Former pitcher

"If you have been sexually active, it's not too late to start over. You can be self-controlled and have your dignity back. You can become abstinent from this point forward."
                                                  Oral Hershiser, Pitcher

"It's definitely worth the wait. There are just too many complications when people cross God's boundaries. He put limitations on us for a reason—to protect us."
                    Lisa, Recording artist in the group Out of Eden

(Celebrity quotes adapted from "Everyone's Doing It?"
Brio magazine, February 1995)

And you thought that everyone was doing it? No way. Tune in to what these teens have to say!

Teen Talk

"I want to be a gift for my husband when I get married. Not one that is already opened, used, and scarred. I came to this decision because I realized I didn't want my husband to be used either. I would feel cheated."   Dawn, 17

"I made a commitment to abstinence because it is a way to show love. I want to show my husband-to-be that I loved him before I ever knew him by remaining pure for him. I want him to be able to trust that I am a faithful person."   Carey, 17

"I'm committed to abstinence not only because God commanded me to, but also because I see all around me the pain and suffering premarital sex causes."   Roni, 16

"A question that often comes up among teens is, 'How far can I go and stay sexually pure?'. That question instead should be rephrased to ask, 'How much of that special gift can I save for that one special person?'"   Ann, 16

"I think one of the greatest gifts of a marriage relationship is the presentation of your pure and unviolated body."
                                                                        Rusty, 17

"Abstinence is God's plan for every guy that is unmarried!"
                                                                        Todd, 18

Your turn! Are you committed to abstinence? What do you think the benefits will be? _____

_____

_____

Tackling Temptations

Making an honest commitment to holding on to your virginity until marriage is HUGE! It's tough, especially when you see romance and love scenes on almost every channel you surf through.

Chances are, you'll need to call for back-up support on this one! Here are a few ideas of help you stand your ground and fight off temptation when it comes your way—and it will! Be ready!

- Restrict your dating to guys who respect God's guidelines as much as you do. When you're both on the same track, the ride is smoother!

- Pray with your guy. Really! Bring God right into the middle of your relationship. Prayer helps fight off temptation and keep your focus on the right stuff.

- Set standards in line with God's standards. Abstaining from sexual intercourse is an absolute, but what about the other stuff? It's important not to do anything that allows you or your guy to become aroused. So, create boundaries! Declare anything below the neck and above the knees off-limits—on your bod as well as his!

- Let small talk lead to big discoveries. Yep. Concentrate on getting to know your guy on the inside! Besides, emotional intimacy is much more fulfilling than physical intimacy.

- More is better! Single dating often allows for situations that are tempting. Double or triple up with other friends. It's much more fun that way, anyhow!

- Don't flirt in a come-on kind of way. Real "babes" don't have to prove they are desirable or attractive. They protect their inner beauty by saying no to anything that will harm the gifts God has given them, including the gift of sex.

Mind Control!

Respect your body and YOUR BRAIN! You can choose to expose your mind only to things that are positive and wholesome! The Book of Proverbs tells us:

Watch over your heart with all diligence
For from it flow the springs of life....
Let your eyes look directly ahead,
And let your gaze be fixed straight in front of you.
Watch the path of your feet,
And all your ways will be established.
Do not turn to the right nor to the left;
Turn your foot from evil.   PROVERBS 23:25-27 (NASB)

We have the task of protecting ourselves from things that cause our thoughts to run wild, flip-flop all over, and potentially produce raunchy thoughts and actions. See, purity (of mind and body) originates inside of us, in our minds! Then it shows in our actions.

What influences should we guard against? Well, just for instance, skim these magazine headline blurbs, "Getting Even with Mom and Dad," "How to Be a Great Gossip," "Firm Your Butt for Him," or "New Makeup Tips for Sexy Eyes." What do revenge, gossip, and using your body to attract guys produce? Big trouble!

TV and movies are just as guilty! The content of most episodes and flicks doesn't come close to being pure and wholesome! Watching those bouncing beauties on *Baywatch*, seeing two *"Friends"* skip into the bedroom to "do it," or witnessing angry dudes delivering pay-backs by blowing people away or by knifing them to death—these are just the type of things to keep *out* of your heart and mind!

Unfortunately we can't erase what we've seen and heard. They leave mind scars!

So, it's up to us to protect ourselves. Yep. We're the ones who have to decide to change the channel, toss out the mag, limit ourselves to Gs and PGs.

Ooh. That's the hard part, huh? You might catch some guff from your friends. You might end up the "odd man out." But you will reap the benefits of using self-control and disciplining your mind and body! In his letter to young Timothy, the apostle Paul encouraged Tim to discipline himself for the purpose of godliness. Using self-control and guarding what gets into your heart and mind leads to godliness. Now that's positive and wholesome!

Let's turn to God's Word. Use these guidelines from Philippians 4:8 (NASB) to help you decide what to allow into your mind.

Can the books, mags, sitcoms, soaps, movies, or song lyrics you see and hear pass this test?

> ★ Is it true?
>
> ★ Is it noble?
>
> ★ Is it right?
>
> ★ Is it pure?
>
> ★ Is it lovely?
>
> ★ It is admirable?
>
> ★ Is it excellent or praiseworthy?

If so, it's a GO!

If not, what are you going to do?

Your Bod Is for God!

Your body and your life are gifts from God! Flip back to chapter one for a mini-refresher course on the fact that God designed and created your body with great love and care. Your body is his work of art!

"You mean God WANTS credit for this body?" You bet! He has big plans for it!

As crazy Christian comedian Ken Davis would say, "GOD WANTS YOUR BODY!"

He does?

Yep.

The Bible says our bodies are "for the Lord" and that we are not our own. We belong to God (1 Corinthians 6:13, 19-20). As an act of our will, we are to give our bodies to God (Romans 12:1)!

For what?

For good deeds! We are God's hands and feet here on earth! It is through us that God reaches out to provide lunch money for a hungry kid, to give someone a ride from school, and to wrap his arms around someone who is hurting. We are the ones God uses to spread some joy at nursing homes or collect canned goods for a homeless shelter.

Ephesians 2:10 confirms this by saying we were created for "good works"!

Just like Jesus shows us in the Gospels, we too can go about doing good! Using our bodies to serve God by serving others is God's plan for us. Yep. Your bod is for God! It's his tool for meeting the needs of those he loves.

List four ways you could do good deeds for your family:

1. _____

2. _____

3. _____

4. _____

How about four awesome ideas for serving your friends?

1. _____

2. _____

3. _____

4. _____

Don't forget about your church and community! List possibilities here!

1. _____

2. _____

3. _____

4. _____

Helping your mom with the ironing, encouraging a friend through her parents' divorce, being a Sunday School helper, visiting with lonely or left-out people, sending notes of thanks to others, or cooking dinner for a stressed-out family are all positive ways to serve and glorify God! I challenge you to respect your body and offer it each day to God to be used for good deeds. You will truly make your Father proud!

BEAUTY BUSTER
Using Your Mouth for Gossip

"My mouth? I suppose that's part of my body I need to control, too!"

Right you are, my friend! That tiny tongue can launch some powerful lies or squelch the most fantastic of fibs.

Yep. We're talking gossip.

Maybe you know someone who runs her mouth as though she were training for an Olympic event! But having leaky lips is no honorable quality. Passing on the grapevine dirt can devastate relationships and destroy reputations. Yes, there is usually a tidbit of truth in the rumors roaming the halls, but certain facts are always missing and other juicy exaggerations get added—in order to make a better story!

The Bible warns us about gossiping and harmful putdowns. We use our mouths respectfully by keeping confidences and cutting off coarse chatter. Check these verses out:

The words of a whisper are like dainty morsels, and they go down into the innermost parts of the body.

PROVERBS 26:22 (NRSV)

A lying tongue hates those it crushes, and a flattering mouth works ruins. PROVERBS 26:28 (NRSV)

He who covers a transgression seeks love, but he who repeats a matter separates intimate friends.

PROVERBS 17:9 (NRSV)

What a shame—yes, how stupid!—to decide before knowing the facts. PROVERBS 18:13 (TLB)

Let no unwholesome word proceed from your mouth, but only such a word as is good for edification according to the need of the moment, that it may give grace to those who hear.

EPHESIANS 4:29 (KJV)

Clearly, God is against gossip! He wants us only to say and repeat things that edify others! To edify means to build someone up, boost their confidence, encourage them. If the words you're about to whisper don't edify, don't say them!

Here are some additional helps for "putting a sock in it," as they say!

1. Turn and walk away. Refuse to listen to gossip.

2. Raise your hand. Signal your friend to stop when she's about to talk about someone else behind their back.

3. Steer clear. Get control of the conversation and turn it in a different direction—away from the gossip.

4. Break your habit. Ask your friends to point out when you slip into gossip. Being aware is half the battle.

5. Call on the Helper. The Holy Spirit will assist you with self-control. Just send up a quick "911-HEAVEN" prayer and he'll be there!

eight

Even the Good, the Bad, and the Ugly?
Understanding God's Unconditional Love

Cindee walked past the front of the picturesque stone church standing proud on the corner of 34th and Lee Lane. She wanted to peer in through the stained glass window, but the dark panes shut her out.

She watched as the others, with freshly pressed dresses and fancy straw hats, filed in through the heavy oak doors that were swung open in a welcoming way.

But Cindee didn't go in.

Turning the corner, she walked along the side of the church, running her fingers along the wrought-iron fence. Eyeing some steps to a separate side entrance, she hoped God wouldn't mind if she sat there. So close to his house, yet on the outside.

"God, I can't go in. I know I have let you down," she whispered.

Cindee knew she had not lived up to what she had been taught was right. She knew she had disappointed the God that had always been so gracious to her.

She was convinced. God must not love her anymore.

After all, how could he? She had pushed him into the closet of her life. She had determined never to stop going to church, but she did. She had not intended on ever liking the smooth taste of fine wine, but she had. She never thought she'd feel the rush from a line of white powder, but she had. And then there was Mark. The memories were almost more than she could bear.

How did life get so messed up? she pondered.

Cindee had done most of the things she never thought she would do. Oh, she hadn't murdered anyone or stolen anything. But in distancing her Lord, she had killed her own self-respect and stolen from herself the confidence she once felt. She was sure God could never forgive her, never love her again.

Jesus loves me, this I know. She could faintly hear the children's song coming from behind the heavy doors. As she strained to listen a tear rolled down her cheek.

I can relate to Cindee's pain.

Years ago, if someone had tenderly taken my face in their hands, looked me straight in the eyes and said, "Andrea, Jesus loves *you*," I wouldn't have believed them. Because of things I had chosen to do, I too wondered if God could really still care for me.

GIRL TALK
Have You Ever Felt
Unworthy of God's Love?

"Yes. Once I read a book that was filled with steamy romance scenes. I felt guilty for allowing those impure thoughts into my mind. But the worst part was, I didn't stop. I read the whole thing! Afterwards, my sin made me feel unworthy of God's pure, holy love for me."   Colleen, 16

> "I was super depressed over my parents' divorce. I tried to drown my feelings by drinking. I even sneaked a bottle of vodka to school. I drank between classes, even poured it in a coke can to hide it. Eventually I got caught and suspended. My parents were furious and very embarrassed. I thought God would hate me. I had made such a wreck. But I know now that he still loves me."
> Abbie, 17
>
> "Yes, when I hurt God by making promises to him that I don't keep or when I put other things in my life before my relationship with him. Then I don't feel lovable and worthy of his continuous love."
> Fawn, 15

What about you?

_____

_____

_____

_____

_____

You see, the truth is, we have all done things that disappoint God. But God doesn't stop loving us. We might feel like he does since we don't fully understand his ability to keep on loving us through the good and the bad!

The Difference Between Human Love and God's Love

We are most acquainted with human love, so we figure God's love is similar. Big mistake! Human love is limited. It is conditional, selfish, incomplete, and sometimes it ends! How about taking a closer look at each of these aspects of human love!

Human love is conditional.

It says "I'll love you if..." If you make straight A's, if you loan me your car, if you sleep with me, if you keep my secret. Conditional love has strings attached. You can only have some people's love if you somehow meet their needs. This kind of love is immature.

Paula insisted that she ride to the class picnic with Jill... until Jill's mom wouldn't let her borrow the car. Suddenly Paula changed plans. Now she was going with a girl from math class, a girl with a brand new, red convertible! Jill was so upset she blew off the picnic and spent the day in her room. Paula's love—that's conditional love.

Human love is selfish.

It's a love that is given depending upon what it can get! It is a love that takes and gives very little in return. Selfish love manipulates others, controlling the circumstances in a situation so that things work out to its advantage.

Maureen only showed up at the home of her aging grandparents on occasion—when she needed some extra cash. She pampered them, hugged them, helped them make dinner, all the while waiting for the perfect moment to ask for the money. Each time she was determined to get what she came for. The eighteen bucks for the concert Saturday night is all she is really thinking about this time. That's selfish love!

Human love is incomplete.

It attempts to love wholeheartedly, but often fails. It holds back. It's the boyfriend who doesn't tell you how he really feels. It's the person who hugs you one minute, then screams at you the next! Incomplete love is often unforgiving. It blames. It holds grudges.

Trudy and Kim were best friends until Kim broke a confidence. She accidentally leaked the truth about the scar on Trudy's cheek. She was so sorry, but to this day, Trudy will not speak to her. That's incomplete, unforgiving love.

Human love can end.

It can die out with the fading of emotions. It changes. It fizzles because it is not committed. It's the parent who walks away, leaving a broken family behind. It's the friend who stops calling. It's the kind of love that disappoints, leaving us sad, lonely, rejected. Love that ends, love that is withdrawn from us, is painful love.

After two years of very steady dating, Curt dumped Marla a month before graduation. The parties, the pictures, the dance, the class trip together—all canceled. Marla felt like her world was crashing in. They had been so tight. She couldn't understand how Curt could do this to her. That's ending love.

Which of these "human loves" have you experienced? Give an example:

_____

_____

_____

_____

_____

_____

_____

_____

Chances are, you and I have had a taste of each of these loves. But would we ever treat our friends or family like this? Never! *Or would we?* Could we be guilty of ever loving others in these ways?

Come on. 'Fess up. I know my love for others has sometimes been conditional, or selfish, maybe incomplete, even withdrawn! My plea: Guilty as charged! But wait. There's a reason!

We are human!

We are surrounded by humans and their human love. We see it in the movies and hear it on the radio. Somebody is always loving 'em, then leaving 'em. Someone always gets hurt, cheated, or mistreated. Ever get the impression that love has to involve pain, broken hearts, and damaged emotions?

The truth is, this is not real love at all. Our world has so distorted real love. Real love involves commitment to another person no matter what the cost. Real love offers security and wholeness. It allows us to be ourselves without the fear of being rejected.

Unconditional love. Unselfish love. Complete and forgiving love. Unending love.

That's God's Love!

God's love is *unconditional!* No strings attached. Conditional love says, "I'll love you if you make the Dean's List." Unconditional love says, "I'll love you even if you *don't* make the Dean's List." Unconditional love doesn't have to be earned. God doesn't love us only if we do everything right. He loves us because we are his. Also because it is his nature to love. See, God doesn't just have love, he *is* love!

God's love is unselfish!

It is a love that gives. And gives. And gives! God's love gives sacrificially. That means it gives its very best. God does not hold back on us. He loves us with all his heart!

God's love is forgiving!

When we ask, God washes away the things we've done wrong. He doesn't keep a record of our mistakes. Yes, we usually have to pay the consequences of our actions, but God does not punish us. His forgiving love never holds grudges, never points at us with a blaming finger!

God's love is unending!

It is eternal, infinite. It has no end! Look up at the sky. It is impossible to see where it ends! As God's children, we can never experience the end of God's love. It keeps going and going and going! God loves us with an everlasting love. It lasts forever!

God loves the reflection you see when you look in your mirror! He loves *you!* All that you are and all that you are not. God has loved you for all eternity; he planned for you, he longed to share his life, his joy, and his love with you!

LOVE QUIZ
Find the Facts About God's Love!

The place to discover more exciting facts about God's love is in the BIBLE! Here's the plan. I'll provide the sentence, you search out the Scripture and fill in the blank. Grab your Bible and dig in!

1. God loves you so much he will never _____ you or _____ you.
   JOSHUA 1:5

2. God's _____ love surrounds the person who trusts him!
   PSALM 32:10 (TLB)

3. God often proves his love through _____.
   HEBREWS 12:5-6

4. List four characteristics of God's love found in 1 Corinthians 13:4-8.

   _____

   _____

5. Since Jesus is the same _____, _____, and _____, that means his love for us is _____.
   HEBREWS 13:8

6. Like a shepherd loves and provides for his sheep, God loves and provides for you! Read Psalm 23. Select two things God provides because he loves you!

   _____

   _____

The greatest proof of God's love for you is Jesus. Let's pick apart the most famous verse in the Bible to see how God's love is revealed in Jesus!

What's the verse?

John 3:16 (KJV)!

> For God so loved the world, that he gave his only begotten Son, that whosoever believeth in him should not perish, but have everlasting life!

God	(The ultimate big guy, ruler of the universe)
so loved	(We're talkin' real love)
the world	(All of us humans living here on planet Earth)
that he gave	(Oh, yes...there's that <u>unselfish</u> love! He gave because he wanted to give; no one forced him)
his only begotten Son	(There it is...<u>sacrificial</u> love! God gave his best and his only! This was a big deal. God doesn't have lots of sons, he has one. Still, he gave him up for us!)
that whosoever	(Aha! <u>Unconditional</u> love! God doesn't love just certain people who meet special requirements. He loves everyone! That's you, me, Cousin Hank, Aunt Myrtle...)
believeth in him should not perish	(Do you see it? It's <u>forgiving</u> love! God loved you so much he sent Jesus to die in your place, to pay the penalty of your sins, so that you could have forgiveness! In Christ you are no longer counted guilty, just forgiven!)
but have everlasting life!	(The grand finale...<u>unending</u> love! Eternal life, that's the kind that lasts into eternity! Upon accepting Jesus' work on the cross, you are no longer doomed to hell, you are heaven-bound! God loves you so much he wants you to be with him forever. That's an everlasting love!)

God loves you so much!

In fact, he's downright crazy about you! God gave his best for you. Jesus willingly gave his *life* for you!

Let's bring this on home!

Put *your* name in the spaces:

God so loved _____,
that he sent his only begotten Son, that (if)
_____ believes in him, she
should not perish, but will have eternal life!

Recently I heard a song that said when Jesus was on the cross, you and I were on his mind. Imagine that! He was thinking about *us*, the ones he was dying for!

Doesn't it feel awesome to know God loves you and loves you a lot?

Whether you are short or tall, pimple-prone or clear-skinned, 450 pounds or 150 pounds, having a good-hair day or a bad-hair day, God loves you!

But does he still love you when you sass your mom, gossip about a friend, lie to a teacher, swipe a pen, flunk a test, or skip out on Sunday School?

Yep.

Definitely.

Incredible, isn't it?

We may feel like we don't deserve his continuing love for us, but he keeps on giving it. Yes, he hates our sin, but loves us. He's God! His love does not give up on us. It's a stubborn love.

GIRL TALK
What Is Your Reaction to This Statement?...

"The One who knows you best (God), loves you most!"

"It gives me the confidence that someone will ALWAYS love me."
Lizza, 13

"I know it's true, but still, it's hard to fathom the depth of God's love."
Jodilyn, 16

"I find this statement humbling. It brings me to my knees."
Ellen, 15

"He knows me so well and still loves me! I find that very comforting."
Mindy, 17

"It reminds me that I don't have to fit into some mold or be something I'm not just so God will love me. With God's love, I can be myself."
Roni, 16

Your turn. Take a few minutes to mull over all we've talked about concerning God's love for you. Now, how do you feel knowing that the God who knows every single teeny-tiny detail of your life, still loves you more than anyone does?

_____

_____

_____

_____

_____

God's love embraces even the worst in us. But it also works in our hearts in such a way that we can become our very best for him.

Before God's love, each of us is like a rosebud. We have our petals closed up! When we experience God's love, we begin to blossom, to open up. His love is like the warmth from the sun and nourishment from the soil. Soon we are in full bloom, showing forth our full beauty, bearing a sweet fragrance unto the Lord.

Our real beauty shines through when we realize just how loved we are. Then we can begin to love ourselves in such a way that we can be our best for the Lord.

His love is very freeing. The truth and reality of God's love set us free. And nothing—no, not one single thing—can separate us from his love.

Here's proof in Scripture:

> For I am convinced that nothing can ever separate us from his love. Death can't, and life can't. The angels won't, and all the powers of hell itself cannot keep God's love away. Our fears for today, our worries about tomorrow, or where we are—high above the sky, or in the deepest ocean—nothing will ever be able to separate us from the love of God demonstrated by our Lord Jesus Christ when he died for us.   ROMANS 8:38-39 (TLB)

GIRL TALK
Nothing Can Separate You from God's Love! Do You Believe It?

"It's hard to comprehend, but I have faith that God's Word is true!"   Ann, 15

"Yes. It gives me a sense of security and assurance that no matter what trials I face or how many times I blow it, God will always love me."   Kate, 14

"I believe this Scripture completely, even though sometimes I don't *feel* his love. But it's never God drawing back from me—it's me drawing back from him. I know God's love is based on facts, not feelings!"   Kristen, 16

There is a very important conclusion I hope you are catching from this chapter.

Are you ready?

Here it is:

YOU ARE WORTH LOVING!

Believing this statement is the key that unlocks your ability to *receive* God's love. God's love is there for you. You have to choose to reach out and snatch hold of it! In my own life, I had to come to understand that I was valuable enough to love.

So do you.

Worthy. Valuable. Important stuff! Stay tuned for more on this in chapter nine!

GIRL TALK
How Do You Show Your Love for God?

"Through my eagerness to learn his Word."   Heidi, 14

"Through music! I think it's very important to praise him because he deserves it."   Leslie, 15

"I try my best to obey what he commands since the Scripture says that if we love him, we will obey him."   Carey, 16

"By going to church and reading my Bible."   Brenda, 13

"I volunteer at a handicapped facility, inner-city project, and crisis pregnancy center. I love him by loving others."   Sabrina, 16

"By standing up for him at school. I always go to 'See You at the Pole' and I speak up on issues like abortion."   Tristin, 15

There are tons of ways to show God you love him! Grab a friend, sister, or your mom, do some brainstorming and come up with five fabulous ways to express your love to God:

1. _____

2. _____

3. _____

4. _____

5. _____

BEAUTY BUSTER
Stomping Out Self-Hate

Having an aversion to yourself is a sure-fire way to blast away at your personal beauty.

Famous preacher Robert Schuller is known for saying:

"Self-disgust leads to self-rust!"

Disgust leads to rust. Rust! You know, that orange-brown crusty stuff that grows on things that aren't *taken care of properly*. Get it?

Self-hate shows in the way a girl fails to take care of herself. Maybe someone has told her that she's worthless, stupid, fat, ugly, and that she will never amount to anything! And the problem is, she believed it! Now she throws herself away with negative behaviors like poor grooming, overeating, sloppy dressing, getting drunk, sleeping around, and blowing off school.

Self-hate also rears its ugly head in a person's relationships. Jesus told us to love others as we love ourselves. This is a big problem for the person dealing with her own self-hate. See, without self-love, a person will not be able to truly love others. Her relationships will be plagued with problems.

Before we can love others we have to love ourselves!

The kind of self-love that Jesus wants us to have is not the conceited, egotistical, big-headed kind. It's a love that has a healthy appreciation for who God has made each of us to be. It's a love for ourselves that understands God's love for us... a love that is based on who we are, not on what we have or haven't done! Loving ourselves is easier when we see ourselves the way God sees us: forgiven, lovable, made in his image, and full of potential!

Take a few minutes to write out a prayer to God, asking him to help you love yourself.

Date _____

Dear Lord,

_____

_____

_____

_____

_____

_____

_____

_____

_____

_____

_____

Yours forever,

nine

Mirror, Mirror, on the Wall, Am I Valuable at All?

Discovering Some Awesome Truths About You!

Brittney and Cassey could think of no better place to spend a Saturday than at the Manchester Mall. It was huge. Three floors of department stores and specialty shops, all packed with sweet sales! There was even a mini-amusement park and a movie theater built right in!

And the food court. Perhaps the toughest decision the girls would face that day would be choosing between pizza, pretzels with cheese, or sweet-and-sour pork! Manchester Mall was definitely the place to be.

Cassey's mom had dropped them off about noon. Since they had already spied the deals at The Gap and 5-7-9, it was break time! A double scoop of pralines and cream in a waffle cone was calling their names.

On the way to the ice cream parlor, Brittney saw Parrotise Alley Pet Shop across the way and insisted they go look at the cockatoos, her favorite bird. Cassey consented. She wasn't into feathered friends! Yet something did catch her attention. Two big round eyes. A fluffy, soft-looking coat of fur. Large paws with short, stubby legs! But those eyes! One was brown, one was blue!

Cassey noticed that there was only one pup of this breed. The original price had been marked out; a new, lower price was written in bright red. On sale! But still big bucks.

"Would you like to pet that puppy?" asked the shop owner.

Cassey stumbled over her words, "Ya, um, if you don't mind. I mean, I can't buy it or anything."

"It's OK. We can't get rid of this one. It's supposed to have two brown eyes. Nobody seems to want it with that blue one. We nicknamed him Big Blue."

The awkward pup licked Cassey's hand, then her face as she picked him up. *This is the sweetest puppy,* Casey thought. *I want this pup, one blue eye and all!*

But the price. Four hundred and fifty-five dollars—ON SALE! How could she ever afford him?

With one last scratch behind his ear, Cassey handed Big Blue back to the owner. Already a plan was forming in her mind. She would take that weekly Saturday babysitting job her aunt had offered, even if it did conflict with her mall excursions. She could also rake yards, maybe even mow. And she could tutor that little Simmons boy in spelling. Maybe if she did extra work around the house, her parents would give her an advance on her allowance!

If she gave it everything she had, Cassey knew that pup could be hers. It would be a sacrifice and she'd have to work fast, but her heart was set.

After three long weeks of hard, sweaty yard work, exhausting hours of keeping up with her little cousins, and seeing Bobby Simmons through the entire alphabet, Cassey finally had the cash she needed to make Big Blue her own.

She marched proudly into the pet shop to purchase her pup. Big Blue stood up when he saw her—tail wagging, ears perked.

She had faithfully visited him, telling him tales of his soon-to-be-home. He was ready!

With great pride and excitement, Cassey carried the floppy fur ball out of the pet shop. No more cramped kennel. No more isolation. Big Blue was going to have a yard to run in, leaves to roll in, and someone to take him on walks, brush his furry coat, and proudly call him her own!

Big Blue was purchased by someone who loved him. Cassey paid a great price; she had to sacrifice in order to save up for her pup. Big Blue became valuable! Before Cassey came along, nobody wanted him. Nobody cared or gave him a chance. That all changed when Cassey came on the scene. Big Blue was valuable to her! She gave him worth.

It's like that between you and God!

You were "purchased" by God! There is no one more worthy and valuable than God himself and he *chose* to take you as his own.

God paid a great price for you! No, not with silver or gold or anything that can lose its worth. He paid by giving Jesus! It was the precious blood of Christ that bought you and me. God wanted us so much he invested all he had. (There's that sacrificial love again!)

Since we were bought by the wealthiest guy around, who paid a very high price (unlike Big Blue, you were not on sale), you are obviously *valuable!*

Your Value "in Christ"

In fact, the Bible explains that you have value because as a Christian you are "in Christ." That means you are part of God's family and the spirit of Jesus (yep, same as the Holy Spirit) lives *in* you!

Because of Jesus, your worth is indescribably high! Not based on your accomplishments, your talents, your looks, your money, your trophies, your popularity, your brand of perfume, the car you drive, the stuff you own, or the good you do. Your value is based on the fact that the King of Kings lives in you!

But who are you "in Christ"? What comes with this position? Let's take a look at God's Word. But you'd better brace yourself! You might discover some awesome things you didn't know!

Totally Awesome Truths About You!

According to **1 Peter 2:9**, you are chosen by God, selected by him, and for him! (Hand-picked by the ultimate Big Guy!)

According to **John 15:15-16**, you are called his friend. (Not a slave, not a neighbor—a friend!)

According to **Ephesians 2:4**, you are loved! (Even when it feels like no one else loves you, know that God does.)

According to **Ephesians 1:5**, you are accepted into God's family. (No more feeling left out—you're in!)

According to **1 John 5:13**, you'll have eternal life in heaven. (What better place to spend forever?)

According to **1 John 1:9**, you are forgiven. (Even when you blow it!)

According to **Ephesians 1:4**, you are holy and blameless in God's sight. (Imagine that! Because of Jesus, God sees you as perfect!)

According to **2 Corinthians 3:15**, your adequacy is from God. (It's not who you are, it's who he is in you!)

According to **Acts 4:13**, your confidence is in Christ when you spend time with him. (There's no better confidence booster than Jesus!)

According to **2 Corinthians 5:17**, you are a new creation in Christ. (God made you new on the inside!)

According to **Philippians 4:13**, you can do all things through Christ. (What God asks you to do, he will help you to do.)

According to **2 Peter 1:3**, you are a partaker of God's divine nature. (You have everything you need to live a godly life.)

According to **Genesis 1:31**, God looked at all he had made and said, "It is very good"—including you! (Wow! God created you with pride.)

According to **Psalms 8:3-5**, you are crowned with glory and majesty. (God's glory, that is!)

According to **Colossians 2:10**, you are complete in Christ. (In Christ you have it all—love, peace, security…)

According to **Romans 8:37**, you are victorious through Christ. (Christ will cause you to come out on top!)

According to **Jeremiah 29:11-13**, your life has a special plan and purpose. (No floundering for you! God has the way paved!)

Are you blown away? Is your hair tousled from the gush of wind? Was I right? Did you discover things about yourself you had no clue were true?

Read through the list again.

Select the verse that impacts or impresses you the most. Write it here: _____

_____

_____

_____

_____

Think about it for a sec. Now, tell me *why* it impacts you.

_____

_____

_____

_____

_____

When you know the value you have in Jesus and what God's Word says about you, your whole life will change!

Mine did!

When the enemy whispered in my ear, "You can't get an A in this course," I whispered back, "Yes, I can! I can do all things because Christ gives me strength."

When he snarled, "Your life is a mess, you're a waste," I boldly proclaimed, "Not true! I'm a new creation in Christ. I am complete in him, and God has a special purpose for my life no matter what it looks like right now."

When he screamed in my face, "You're a rotten Christian! In fact, you probably aren't even a *real* Christian. Besides, why would God want you?" I knew what God's Word said about me, so I confidently snapped back to that dirty devil, "You're wrong! I am chosen by God, and I have eternal life. Plus, Christ's nature in me provides me with everything I need to live like a Christian. And if I blow it, God forgives me. The Bible says so!"

Has Satan ever tried to make you doubt *your* value? Sometimes he uses other people to make cutting comments to you. Sometimes he rubs your mistake in your face. Don't let him do it! Arm yourself with God's Word! When you know what is true about you, you can fight off Satan's fiery darts!

Knowing who you are and what you have because of your position in Christ gives your whole outlook on life a God-sized *boost!*

The Way to True Beauty:
A Christ-Like Heart

But wait. There's more. There is a *purpose* for all of this.

When the Holy Spirit unpacks his bags and calls your body home sweet home, he brings with him the inner qualities and characteristics that will give *you* a Christ-like heart.

Romans 8:29 clues us in on God's top priority: *We are to be like Jesus!* God desires for us to have a Christ-like heart.

Check out 1 Samuel 16:7 (NAS).

> God sees not as man sees, for man looks at the outward appearance, but the Lord looks at the heart!

According to God, your appearance doesn't reveal your true value (or your true beauty).

It's your heart that counts.

So, how can we have a Christ-like heart?

I've got the answer! (You didn't think I'd leave you hangin', did you?) You can have a Christ-like heart by allowing the Holy Spirit to produce his fruit in you! Yep. Once you put God in control of your life the Holy Spirit goes to work building the characteristics and qualities of Christ into your heart!

Then, these inner characteristics and qualities show up in the way you live—what you say and do! This gives you even more value. You are bursting with value!

Oh, what *are* these "fruits" or qualities? Guess where you can find them? That's right! In God's Word. Flip open to Galatians 5:22-23 to see with your own two baby blues (or browns or hazels). Here are nine of the qualities, complete with definitions, that make yours a Christ-like heart:

Love

Christ-like love is the God-kind of love! That means choosing to really love unconditionally, no strings attached, even if you are not loved in return. Human love empowered by the Holy Spirit moves us toward the God-kind of love. We can love like he does!

Joy

Christ-like joy is more than putting on a happy face. It is a deep trust that God is in control, even if life seems to be going nuts! Therefore, you can smile no matter what.

Peace

Christ-like peace shows contentment and confidence in God. You can be worry-free! Imagine, "hakuna matata"! No worries!

Patience

Under pressure? Feel like throwing a fit? Christ-like patience remains calm, without complaining, even when life's not going at the pace you prefer!

Kindness

Even if you have been mistreated, Christ-like kindness will help you treat others in a gentle, tenderhearted way, seeking the best for others.

Goodness

Christ-like goodness chooses to be morally good, upholding godly standards, in spite of the world's attitudes like—"Who cares?", "There's no right or wrong," or "Everybody's doing it."

Faithfulness

Tempted to quit? Give up? No way! Christ-like faithfulness follows through, finding encouragement in Jesus to keep from growing weary while choosing to do the right thing.

Gentleness

Christ-like meekness doesn't plaster its accomplishments on a billboard—it shows humility, giving glory to God.

Self-control

Christ-like self-control keeps you from doing and saying stuff that would not please the Lord! It is true *inward* strength.

There they are. These Christ-like characteristics are available to you seven days a week, twenty-four hours a day! In fact, you can call on the Holy Spirit to supply you with them just when you need them.

GIRL TALK
Share a Time When the Holy Spirit Gave You What You Needed Right When You Needed It.

"Once a friend of mine received an award at school that I thought I was going to receive. Satan tried to fill me with bitterness, jealousy, and embarrassment, but thankfully, the Holy Spirit supplied me with gentleness, kindness, love, and joy towards my friend; peace and patience that it was all part of God's plan; self-control to stop the thoughts and attitudes I was tempted with. I'm so glad the Holy Spirit is *always* with me."
                                                          Leslie, 15

"When my aunt died, it was a sad and tough time for my family. But the day before the funeral we all started telling our favorite stories about her and we laughed and laughed! The Holy Spirit gave us joy in the midst of our sorrow."
                                                          Krista, 14

"Last year all my friends had dates to our school Valentine's Dance, except me! I moped while they made plans. But then the Holy Spirit gave me peace. He helped me realize his timing is perfect and someday he will provide me with a boyfriend."
                                                          Sabrina, 16

"On our mission trip to Mexico, the people were dirty and smelled awful. The little kids had dried snot on their faces and flies all around them. At first it was hard, but I prayed and the Holy Spirit gave me an incredible love for them. I was even able to hug them and really mean it!"
                                                          Raina, 14

As you spend time with God through prayer and Bible reading, you'll see each of these fruits of the Spirit blossoming in your heart.

A Christ-like heart is your source of true beauty. Being a loving, joyful, patient, kind person *is* what makes you absolutely attractive! That's the Bible's kind of beauty!

1 Peter 3:4 instructs us to be beautiful on the *inside*, in our H-E-A-R-T-S! That's where it really matters!

A beautiful heart is a Christ-like heart. Here is a list of tried and true ideas to help you be even more like Christ:

★ Smile at those who are rude to you!

★ Work out to Christian videos!

★ Let go of grudges!

★ Stand up for what is right!

★ Write out your prayers in a journal!

★ Don't gossip—zip your lip!

★ Let someone else go first!

★ Choose Christian friends who have morals similar to yours!

★ Get involved at church!

★ Keep your promises!

★ Give three compliments a day!

★ Sing praise songs in the shower and the car!

★ Put on a "gospel" puppet show for your neighborhood kids!

★ Memorize Scripture—tape verses in your locker!

★ Listen to music that encourages a Christ-like attitude!

★ Respect your parents!

★ Don't dwell on sinful thoughts!

★ Ask yourself, "What would Jesus do?"

★ Get involved in a small group Bible study!

★ Invite a friend to youth group!

★ Read one chapter of the New Testament every day!

★ Look for the *good* in others!

★ Don't go places you wouldn't want to take Jesus!

★ Be honest!

★ Bake cookies for someone special!

★ Befriend someone who is alone!

★ Add your ideas:

_____

_____

_____

_____

_____

_____

_____

The facts are final:

**You are valuable to God
because Christ is in you!**

Did you notice all the prime words from this chapter started with "P"? See if you can fill in the blanks!

MINI-QUIZ

1. You were _____ by God.

2. The _____ he paid was Jesus' precious blood.

3. Your _____ as a child of God is "in Christ."

4. God's _____ for the Holy Spirit living in you is to create a Christ-like heart!

Answers: 4. Purpose; 3. Position; 2. Price; 1. Purchased.

Uncover Your Power-Packed Potential!

Add these together and you get **potential!**

That's right. The valuable gal you are is full of potential! You are free to be yourself. Your confidence is in Christ. Your adequacy is from God. Your life has a plan! You are gifted. You are talented!

Did you know God himself gives gifts and talents to each of his kids? Some are natural talents and tendencies that he gives you at birth (like the ability to sing, draw, or write poetry).

Some are specific gifts given to us by the Holy Spirit as God sees fit (like the ability to teach the Bible, encourage others, lead groups, or organize activities).

Let's do a little detective work! Examine this list of gifts and talents. Ask yourself, "Which gifts do I have?"

Circle the things you are good at. Also take note of the areas you excel in or really enjoy.

Ready? Start diggin'!

comforting a hurting classmate

playing a musical instrument

singing

individual sports

writing stories, songs, poems

chemistry experiments

drawing, painting

hairstyling

sewing

writing letters to penpals
    and missionaries

computers

teaching children's church

helping others understand
    their homework

raising money for a worthy cause

helping others accomplish their goals

believing God can do the impossible

buying necessities for others

dividing up the household chores

leading a Bible study

team sports

acting

dance

fixing things

baking

making others feel special

gardening

making others laugh

class officer duties

organizing a project

praying for friends

sending encouraging notes

giving clothes to the needy

mathematics

identifying with others' feelings

sharing the Gospel with non-believers

Others that come to mind _____

_____

_____

_____

_____

1. List four things at which you *excel*:

_____

_____

_____

_____

2. Jot down five things you *enjoy* doing:

_____

_____

_____

_____

_____

3. Record three things that are unique about you:

_____

_____

_____

Are you catching any clues as to what your gifts and talents are? Do you see any patterns forming? Any correlations?

Scrutinize all your answers. With an investigative edge, what conclusions can you draw about your God-given gifts and talents?

_____

_____

_____

_____

_____

No more Chameleon Syndrome for you! You know, that's when you try to change to fit in with the crowd or when you try to be what someone else wants you to be.

You are free to be the person God has called you to be! He has packed you full of potential. He has blessed you with specific gifts and talents. We are equally gifted, equally valuable to God! He gives us gifts and talents based on the plan he has for our lives. They will help us accomplish God's goals for us!

You can put your gifts and talents to good use for the Lord's service. That's using your value in a valuable way! Heather Whitestone, Miss America 1995, did this very thing!

Up Close and Personal
with Heather Whitestone, Miss America 1995

"Anything is possible with God's help!" That's the personal motto of Heather Whitestone, who was crowned Miss America 1995, after performing a perfectly executed ballet to music she couldn't hear.

Heather is deaf!

At just eighteen months of age, Heather suffered a rare complication from a childhood vaccination. The medicine the doctors prescribed to cure her left her profoundly deaf.

The reality of her condition brought her face to face with God and his plan for her life.

"I cried a lot in high school. I was angry at God, and I remember asking him to make me hear again."

That wasn't God's plan. But Heather found hope and encouragement from the Bible, learning that God has a purpose for everything and that he can be trusted.

"I've told God so many times that I don't choose to be deaf," Heather says. "But if he can use my deafness to change other people's lives, then I will be deaf for him. My deafness forces me to depend on God more."

Heather is proof that listening to God involves more than perfect hearing! Though her deafness has been a challenge to her, Heather chose to put her gifts and talents to use for God.

In fact, Heather sees her deafness as a different kind of gift. She believes God has given each of us gifts and it's our responsibility to use them for him!

Heather put in hundreds of hours at the dance studio to perfect yet another gift: Dance! That very gift helped open the door to winning the royal crown!

Heather believes that becoming Miss America was God's chosen way for her to put her God-given gifts to work for him! She's also confident that he has a special plan for *your* gifts and talents, too!

Since Psalm 148:3 calls us stars, Heather created a five-point plan (like the five points on a star) to encourage others to use their gifts and talents for the Lord!

1. **Think positively.** Remember, with God's help you can do it!

2. **Dare to dream.** Pray, find God's goal for your life, and go for it!

3. **Be willing to work hard.** Give God nothing less than your best!

4. **Face your obstacles.** See obstacles as opportunities to find new solutions to tough situations!

5. **Build a support team.** Surround yourself with caring adults who will affirm and pray for you!

With your hand in God's hand, together you can discover, develop, and put your gifts and talents to use for him! A final note from Heather:

Pray! Trust God! Be patient! Anything is possible!

(Adapted from "Heather Whitestone: A Deaf Ear to Success,"
Brio magazine, August 1995.)

ten

Beauty from the Inside Out!
Inner Qualities Bursting with Beauty

Geode. Strange name. Strange rock!

Traveling from our home to visit my family in Tulsa, Oklahoma, Bill and I took a mini-detour to Eureka Springs, Arkansas. Nestled in the Ozark Mountains, this quaint little town is full of unique stores.

Naturally, I couldn't help myself!

I had to shop!

It happened in the third, maybe fourth store we'd been in (my husband is such a sport!). A sparkle caught my eye. Being a former pageant contestant, I'm drawn to things that sparkle: beaded gowns, shiny crowns, rhinestone jewelry! But a glimmer of glitz here in a rock shop?

I walked closer.

A beautiful layer of purple-toned jewels, embedded in a layer of clear, glassy matter, all attached to a... dull, gray rock? Quite a phenomenon. It's called a geode. It is a hollow body of stone lined with mineral crystals that grow toward the center or inner-most part of the stone.

To look at the hard, grayish outside of the geode, it appears to be an ordinary rock. No two rocks look exactly the same, but nevertheless, a geode just looks like a plain ol' rock.

But the *inside* is a different story. My geode (yep, I had to buy one) is filled with brilliant lavender colored crystals. This is where we get the semi-precious gem called amethyst (the official birthstone of you February babes).

Precious Gems of Inner Beauty

As I pondered this geode, turning it from one side to the other and back again, it occurred to me that we, as Christians, should be like this rock! It isn't our outsides that are to be polished and prissy, drawing the attention of others. It is our insides.

When people look at us, God wants them to find precious gems of *inner* beauty!

People found gems of inner beauty in Jesus! The disciples and the crowds that followed him did not like him because he was muscular or cute! Jesus wasn't a suave, macho kind of guy who tried to win people over to God's kingdom with good looks. In fact, rumor has it, in spite of his popularity, Jesus wouldn't have exactly qualified for the cover of *GQ!*

How do I know that? The Bible gives us just one glimpse into the appearance of our Lord.

> He had no beauty or majesty to attract us to him, nothing in his appearance that we should desire him. ISAIAH 53:2 (NIV)

It wasn't Jesus' physical attractiveness that drew others to him, it was his *inward* attractiveness! He was filled with precious gems of inner beauty.

Too cool! Jesus may have been dull on the outside, but he was dynamite on the inside!

GIRL TALK
What Is Inner Beauty?

"Following the Golden Rule spelled out in Matthew 7:12: 'Do unto others as you would want them to do to you.'"

Carron, 14

"Doing good things in secret because of your love for God, not just because it might make you look good."   Fawn, 15

"Being loyal, trustworthy, and dependable!"   Carey, 17

"Inner beauty is a quality that fills a person, spilling onto the outside, making her beautiful on the outside, too."   Dela, 14

"A person who loves the Lord, others, and herself (in that order) will be beautiful on the inside."   Michelle, 18

"Inner beauty is having a solid confidence in your relationship with the Lord, allowing you to put effort into building up others instead of yourself."   Ann, 18

"Allowing God to mold your thoughts and feelings to his own, so that his love shows in everything you do."   Toni, 18

"Inner beauty is having character. You don't fall apart when things don't turn out the way you planned. You trust that God will work everything out in his own time, so you can go through life without bitterness or holding grudges."

Dawn, 16

And what about you? Describe inner beauty:

_____

_____

_____

_____

_____

Beauty on the inside is beauty that matters! Did you notice, not one of these teens said that inner beauty had anything to do with appearance? That's because inner beauty—true beauty—is not based on what you look like!

Good thing, too!

In case you haven't already noticed this by looking at those around you, the Bible keys us in to an important fact of life. It's there in black and white in 2 Corinthians 4:16: **Outer beauty fades**!

Yep. As a woman ages, her youthful appearance begins to melt away! Eyes droop, hair dulls, muscle tone sags (just to point out a *few* of the changes!).

But hey—does it really matter anyway? Is it your physical body that you're going to take with you into eternity? No! It's your inner person (gifted with a new, heavenly body) that will last forever.

So where would be the wisest place to focus our time and attention?

Right! Inner beauty!

Listen up:

> Be beautiful inside, in your hearts, with the lasting charm of a gentle and quiet spirit which is so precious to God. 1 PETER 3:4 (TLB)

Wow! Inner beauty is lasting. Did you catch that part about a gentle and quiet spirit? That must be extremely important if God himself calls it precious!

The Beauty of a Gentle and Quiet Spirit

We'd better dig into this gentle and quiet stuff! I can imagine your questions: *Does gentle mean I can't rough around with my brother or play squash ball at youth group? Does it mean I can't run track or be winded and sweaty? Does quiet imply tiptoeing through life trying not to make noise? Does it mean I can't blast my CD's or laugh really hard and loud? Does it mean I have to be... BORING?*

STOP before you scare yourself!

This verse isn't talking about your personality traits or your personal likes and dislikes. Gentle and quiet are references to the condition of your *spirit!*

To be gentle-spirited is a result of knowing you are loved and accepted by God (which you already know you are). It's a humble understanding that to him you are very valuable. Therefore, you are able to genuinely treat others with kindness and tenderness. A girl with a gentle spirit shows mercy and forgiveness toward others.

A gentle spirit! What a wonderful inner beauty quality. No wonder it is precious to God!

What about this *quiet* business? To be quiet of spirit means to be inwardly calm and peaceful. This is the spirit of a girl who is prayed up! She has placed her cares and concerns into God's hands (remember, he has BIG hands that can handle *all* your concerns). Because the quiet spirit trusts the Lord, it is not easily ruffled or disturbed by the surprises and disappointments that are a natural part of life here on planet Earth!

God cherishes a quiet spirit! It is an inner beauty trait that he values.

What do you get when you add a gentle spirit with a quiet spirit?

I know, it looks like a setup, but it's really not a trick question.

Mix together a pinch of gentle and a dash of quiet and you get a young lady who is *content!* Content with her God, herself, her life!

Gracie was one content gal! No fancy house, didn't even own a car, glad to just have those boiled potatoes with dry bread for dinner. Gracie's contentment showed up in the fact she never complained and whimpered about her clothes or her hair or her—oh, I'm sorry. Who is Gracie? Let me formally introduce you!

Several years ago, Bill and I ventured out with six of our youth group kids to Narok, Kenya on a short-term mission trip. We were scheduled to do work projects for the Maasai tribe.

The majority of the Maasai people are still quite primitive. Most of them dress in traditional colored blankets and decorative sheets which they wrap and tie around their bodies. They are shepherds by trade, walking everywhere they go (usually barefoot), and some even carry spears!

Well, we had been working on building a corn bin in one of the bush communities for several days when a girl named Gracie invited Keri (my teen teammate) and me to her home.

Keri, longing for the luxury of her bedroom back home, was anxious to see how Gracie had decorated her room. She wondered if her bedspread would be floral or striped and what posters she would have on her walls.

Gracie led us down a narrow trail through trees and bushes to an area that was surrounded by a fence of sticks. We walked through the crooked gate and there before us were five small huts made of sticks packed with a mud-manure mixture!

Gracie was so excited as she ran toward the second hut and motioned us in. We ducked down to get in the small doorway. Four steps into the dark hut, our eyes were hit with the sting of smoke. Our lungs were a bit stunted as well.

The smoke was from a small, ongoing campfire in the center of the dirt floor, used for cooking and light. There were no windows for the smoke to escape.

"This is where I sleep," Gracie smiled. We glanced over to see a piece of dried cowhide stretched over a bed of branches, set a foot above the ground. No mattress. No pillow. No bedspread.

And Gracie didn't sleep there alone. Her three younger siblings shared the sleeping space with her.

Posters on the wall? No. Just a single sheet of newspaper she had found one day in the village.

Pretty barren.

"Well, where do you keep all your stuff?" Keri asked.

Gracie reached under the bed, pulling out a little trunk. Lifting the lid, she proudly pulled out two tattered dresses, a pair of rubber shoes, a Bible, and some school supplies.

That was it. Everything she owned.

She was so happy to have it!

And so excited to show it to us. These were the prized possessions God had blessed her with.

That night in our tent, Keri was very quiet. Finally, in a small voice, she spoke.

"I promise to never again complain about my clothes or my bedroom or wanting my own phone line. I want to be thankful for what I have."

Keri was moved by the happiness Gracie exuded when she owned so little. See, Gracie was content! She was graciously willing to accept what God had given her. She was grateful to him for loving her and providing for her needs. Her little trunk looked so empty, yet her heart was so full!

Contentment is an inner beauty quality. It leads to an attitude of gratitude, not grumpitude (OK, I made up that word). How do you currently rate on the contentment scale?

Consider these questions, then rate yourself:

CONTENTMENT QUIZ:
Are You Gracious or Grumpcious?

1. Do you feel peaceful about the way your life is going?

   O   1   2   3   4   5   6   7   8   9   10

   DISCONTENTED   CONTENTED

2. Does your stomach turn every time you see someone who just got their license show up in a brand-new car?

   O   1   2   3   4   5   6   7   8   9   10

   DISCONTENTED   CONTENTED

3. Do you wish you could get your hair to look the way someone else's does?

   O   1   2   3   4   5   6   7   8   9   10

   DISCONTENTED   CONTENTED

4. Are you satisfied with the special body God has given you?

   O   1   2   3   4   5   6   7   8   9   10

   DISCONTENTED   CONTENTED

5. Do you feel anxious about going to Mark's sixteenth birthday party, especially since you couldn't afford a new outfit?

   O   1   2   3   4   5   6   7   8   9   10

   DISCONTENTED   CONTENTED

6. Would you be excited to hear you were going to Grandma's again on vacation, or would you feel cheated that you weren't at Disney World or Bahama-bound?

O   1   2   3   4   5   6   7   8   9   10
DISCONTENTED   CONTENTED

7. Have you ever avoided bringing your friends to your house because of where it was and what it looked like?

O   1   2   3   4   5   6   7   8   9   10
DISCONTENTED   CONTENTED

8. Do you get seriously bummed-out when you don't get the privileges other teens do like late curfew, class trips, or private telephone lines?

O   1   2   3   4   5   6   7   8   9   10
DISCONTENTED   CONTENTED

So, in general, are you content? Do you see room for improvement? Need to banish grumpitude and expand your gratitude? Take a tip from Gracie and be glad for what God has given you, no matter how much or how little!

Contentment is very valuable quality because it leads to yet another inner beauty quality: **joy!**

A Joyful Person Is a Beautiful Person!

When joy is bubbling deep within you, it stirs up and produces some terrific stuff!

First of all, joy makes you feel better. Get this! The Bible says a merry, cheerful, joyful heart acts like a medicine to our bodies (Proverbs 17:22). Joy and laughter bring healing to our physical ailments. Science has backed this up! It's been proven that a certain chemical is released into our bloodstream when we laugh or have a joyful attitude. This chemical triggers health! It strengthens the immune system. A joyful person is less likely to become sick in the first place. Not only does their joy keep them out of the doctor's office, it helps others! Joy spreads! If you are joyful, you can't help but splash some onto someone else!

Second, joy gives us strength—joy in the Lord, that is (look it up in Nehemiah 8:10)! Joy gives us mental, emotional, and physical strength (of course, not the same physical strength that comes from pumping up your muscles at the gym).

Joy provides *stamina* and determination to carry on when life has dropped a big load in our arms. Joy gives us courage to stay strong when we feel like crumbling into a corner to cry! Joy sustains us when we're so tired of thinking!

Joy can do all of this when it is founded in Christ. Since we know we rate with God and that he is with us all—not part but all—of the time, we can have joy!

The psalmist instructs us to delight ourselves in the Lord (Psalm 37:4). That means to find our joy in him!

How do we really do that? How do we find everything we need in Christ?

Inquiring minds want to know!

Where in the world can we find the answers to these questions?

We can't. That's the point.

In the *world*, you can't find answers, but in the *Word* you can!

So let's head over to Proverbs. I've heard about a woman there who might be able to help us. She's described throughout chapter 31. But it's verse 30 (TLB) that sums up what we're searching for.

Charm can be deceptive and beauty doesn't last, but a woman who fears and reverences God shall be greatly praised.

Did you catch it?

What is it that can help us develop lasting beauty?

What can help us be joyful?

What can cause our every need to be met?

Fear and **reverence!**

More simply put, honor and respect the Lord! That comes as we develop our relationship with him. Prayer, Bible reading, depending on God, putting Jesus first in your life, all these develop your relationship with the Lord.

Honoring and respecting the Lord—that makes a woman truly beautiful!

TEEN TALK
Describe a Woman in Your Life Who Is Truly Beautiful

"My mother. She's sensitive, funny, tolerant, pleasant, thoughtful, hard-working, and talented!"   Rebeccah, 15

"Mary Anne, a woman at my church. She's been teaching the children's 'good news' for years. She has a true servant's heart, rarely receives praise, yet never seems to get discouraged. She must be aiming for a heavenly goal."   Kristen, 16

"My fifth grade Sunday School teacher was the most beautiful person I know. She made me realize my heart was more important than my appearance. She inspired me to have a personal walk with Christ."   Sabrina, 16

"My mom! She has a heart for the Lord! She has always been a good influence on me and has helped me make the right choices."   Brad, 17

"My friend Evelyn comes to mind immediately! She has suffered many difficulties and looks at hardships as learning experiences. She truly trusts that God is in control. She loves people and generously sows into their lives."   Dawn, 17

"Debbie, a friend of my mom's, has always treated me with unconditional love. I can be honest and upfront with her and she never thinks less of me. She daily reads her Bible because she really wants to learn more about God, which is great because she always shares with me what she is learning."
Jordan, 16

WOW! Women who love the Lord are incredible. They inspire us to keep developing our relationship with him!

Did you notice all the good things the women mentioned did for others? That's a big part of being inwardly attractive. The time we give to others—whether it's a brother or sister or a volunteer in a hospital—as well as the special things we do for others—send a big message about our inner beauty. The woman described in Proverbs 31 was oozing with beauty from the inside out! Let's see what is said about her.

Praise her for the many fine things she does. These good deeds of hers shall bring her honor and recognition from even the leaders of the nations.   PROVERBS 31:31 (TLB)

What is this gracious woman known for?

Fine things!

Good deeds!

My mom always told me that "Pretty is, what pretty does!" Pretty is not what you *look* like, it's what you *act* like. Your inner beauty is displayed by the fine things and good deeds you do! That's the beauty of a Proverbs 31 gal!

Up Close and Personal
with 1997 Brio Girl
Lindy Morgan

When asked what message she would like to share with other teenage girls, sixteen-year-old Lindy Morgan had this to say:

"Proverbs 31:30-31 are such important verses! And they were written just for us!

"So, what do they mean? Verse 30 means that sometimes we get so wrapped up in our outward appearance, but that is not what God cares about! He cares what is in your heart a hundred times *more* than what is on the outside! Charm *is* deceitful, beauty *doesn't* last!

"Plus, we are guaranteed that a woman who honestly fears and reverences the Lord will be greatly praised. That's in verse 31!

"I really feel like that means when we take our focus off of ourselves and put in on the Lord, everything else pales in comparison! Even a bad-hair day!

"The greatest praise any of us could ever receive would be praise from the Lord! It could come in the form of an answered prayer, a sense of peace, or just feeling God saying, 'Well done, woman of the Lord. I love you. I made you and you're really beautiful to me.'"

QUIZ:
Are You a Proverbs 31 Kind-a-Gal?

Are you on your way to fitting the description of the famous Proverbs 31 woman? We'll omit the hubby and kiddy facts and get right to the ones that apply to you!

Before you begin, read Proverbs 31:10-31!

1. A friend asks you to turn in her History assignment for her. She
   A. knows you will do it.
   B. figures there is a 50/50 chance you'll remember.
   C. mails in a copy just in case.

2. You're planning a party. You
   A. get busy decorating, baking brownies, and creating new dips for the chips.
   B. pay your younger sister to do most of the work.
   C. hold the party at a restaurant.

3. Your teacher asks the class to save their book reports to be turned in again at the year's end. You
   A. create a file labeled "English Book Reports," drop in the report, and neatly place the folder in your file cabinet.
   B. toss it on top of your desk with all your other papers.
   C. give it to a friend to copy, never to see it again.

4. You need to upgrade your computer. You
   A. investigate the market looking for the one that is just right, then save up to buy it.
   B. listen intently to the cute salesman and ask which one he likes, then put it on layaway.
   C. have your dad pick it out; after all, he's buying.

5. Your mom is having a hard time lifting the sacks of potting soil from the trunk. You
   A. lift them for her.
   B. offer to carry one end.
   C. suggest she wait until dad or big brother gets home.

6. You saw the cutest dress today at the mall but it's expensive. You
   A. make a similar one for half the cost.
   B. wait until it goes on sale.
   C. ask for an allowance advance and buy it immediately.

7. Your youth group is scheduled to work at the soup kitchen the same day you had planned to go to the art fair. You
   A. wholeheartedly choose to help those less fortunate.
   B. work at the soup kitchen for an hour, then take off for the fair.
   C. head to the art fair and plan to pray for the poor.

8. Your brother trips down the steps in the dark carrying an arm-load of hockey gear to the basement. You say:
   A. "I would be glad to help you next time, or at least let me get the light for you."
   B. "That's what you get for trying to do it all yourself."
   C. "What a lamebrain."

9. It's your responsibility to fold towels this week. You
   A. fold them ASAP.
   B. let them sit in the basket for two days.
   C. ignore them until your mom threatens you.

10. Nicole is having a sleepover Saturday night after the school dance. You:
    A. pass on the sleepover so you don't miss Sunday School and church.
    B. sleep over and blow off Sunday School, but you make it to church.
    C. sleep over and sleep in.

Scoring this quiz is easy!

If you answered mostly A's, you get the Proverbs Kind-a-Gal Award! You have a good grasp of working hard, being organized, serving others, and loving the Lord. You are on the inner-beauty fast track!

If you answered mostly B's, you get the Up-and-Coming Award! You are on your way to becoming a Proverbs Princess. Beware of falling prey to compromising your goals, your values, and your relationship with the Lord.

If you answered mostly C's—Proverbs Alert! You tend to be self-focused, quick to take the easy way out, and unconcerned about spiritual things. Read over the A answers to get a clear picture of some better choices. Just don't give up! God won't give up on you!

Here's another verse to tuck away in your heart:

> Christian women should be noticed for being kind and good, not for the way they fix their hair or because of their jewels or fancy clothes.   1 TIMOTHY 2:9-10 (TLB)

There it is! Straight from the pages of the oldest, yet the wisest and best-selling book of all time!

Ask yourself: When others think of you, do they think of your kindness, good deeds, servant attitude, and caring actions? Or do they say things like...

"Oh, that Betsy, she always has the coolest clothes."

"Karen's hair is to die for! Did you see how she has it styled today?"

If people think of your outer beauty before your inner beauty, it's time to do a 180-degree turn! Being known for being kind and good brings honor to God.

"Sue is always busy helping those kids from the shelter."

"Have you noticed Krista never goes first at lunch?"

"I heard Missy was the only one who stayed after youth group to help clean up."

"Guess what? Deb is forfeiting our senior trip to go to Mexico and build a school for some poor kids."

"Lisa is always so nice to old Mrs. Hankins."

Kind and good! That's what you're to be known for! You can do it!

BEAUTY BUSTER
"Me! Me! Me!"

Call it what you like: self-seeking, self-interested, self-absorbed, self-centered. But the bottom line for such people is that little word: *self!*

A selfish, greedy person who hoards possessions and only looks out for "Number One" is a person void of inner beauty. Barren. Desolate. Dried up. Dusty. Get the picture? A heart without inner beauty is like a desert!

Don't let it be said that your heart is like a desert. Water it daily with a giving, caring, and sharing attitude. Be like Jesus. He said he came to serve, not to be served. He was unselfish. Since we are to be like him, we'd be wise to roll up our sleeves, tie back our hair, and pitch in!

Prove your servanthood by letting your actions speak for themselves—and by slipping in a few random acts of kindness! If you get stuck after coming up with one or two, run down this list to get your good deed juices flowing!

Random Acts of Kindness!

1. Refill the empty Kleenex boxes around the house.
2. Sweep the patio and wipe down the furniture.
3. Shock your mom by volunteering to make dinner.
4. Put the morning newspaper outside your dad's bedroom door.
5. Empty all the wastebaskets in your house.

6. Send a piece of candy back to the teller at your drive-through bank.

7. Slip a note of appreciation into your friend's school bag.

8. Bake a few dozen chocolate chip cookies, then give one dozen to each of the elderly people on your street.

9. Weed the garden or flower bed.

10. Smile and say "hi" to six people you don't know.

11. Let someone else go first in the movie line.

12. Volunteer to pass out bulletins at church.

13. Gather up all the winter clothes you don't wear, then donate them to Goodwill or a local shelter before the weather gets cold.

14. Ride bikes, shoot hoops, or play dolls or a card game with your bored siblings!

15. Add your creative ideas here:

BEAUTY BONUS
Smart Shopping Tips!

Being a smart shopper is an art worth developing. Proverbs 31:14-18 suggests that a woman who is a smart shopper searches out good buys and considers a purchase before she buys it. She is *not* an impulsive buyer. She seriously thinks through the practicality, value, and appropriateness of an outfit. She asks herself: Do I need this? Is this worth spending my (or my parents') money on? Does this outfit fit my lifestyle? Do I already own something like this? A smart shopper *thinks* before she acts.

Here are twelve tips to help you spend less money and less time in your closet trying to figure out what to wear.

1. **Know the difference between a classic style and a fad.**
Classic style clothes don't go in and out of fashion from season to season. Examples include jeans, vests, turtlenecks, and straight-lined skirts. Fads are those unique, flashy, or funky styles that are popular for only a short time. To avoid wasting money, add only one or two fads to your wardrobe per season.

2. **Study designer lines so you can find well-made look-alikes** for about half the cost.

3. **Choose three to five of your favorite colors** from your "season" (cool shades or warm shades), then expand from there. This will give you mix-n-matchability.

4. **Check your mood before you buy.** If you're in a wild, upbeat mood, you may buy something you'll never be brave enough to wear in public! If you're down in the dumps, you may buy dull, dark-colored, baggy clothes that you won't want to wear once you snap out of it.

5. **Shop for quality, not quantity.** Well-made clothes will last longer and end up being the better deal. Check the buttons, zippers, and seams. Lined clothes will also hold up better. Sometimes you really can get great deals, but think twice.

   Is an item on the sale rack because it wouldn't sell? Is it off-colored, damaged, or soon to be out of style? It may not be a bargain after all.

6. **Avoid overbuying on the same item.** You probably don't need six different pairs of jeans or fifteen T-shirts. Be sure your wardrobe is well-rounded so you'll have the appropriate attire for every occasion.

7. **Plan ahead on prints and plaids.** As a general rule, and especially for a limited budget, decide to buy solid bottoms (pants, skirts, shorts) and printed tops or vice versa. It looks best to select designs that correlate to your body size. A girl with a large frame will appear larger wearing a tiny flowered print, while a small-framed girl will look swallowed up in an oversized pattern.

8. **Purchase clothes when you are with one trusted friend or a parent.** It's too difficult to make smart shopping decisions when *everyone* in your group is giving you her opinion.

9. **Choose easy-to-care-for fabrics.** Cottons and cotton/polyester blends don't require the extra cost of dry cleaning. Select fabrics that work well together. Tops and bottoms should have a similar feel to them: dressy with dressy, casual with casual.

10. **Shop for complete outfits.** You won't have to worry about finding something to go with that one new piece later.

11. **Select clothes that fit your clothing personality.** Most females are strong in one clothing style and dabble in one or two others. Which one are you?

The classic personality:
> You feel your best in tailored, timeless styles.

The dramatic personality:
> You go for the exotic fashion extremes.

The sporty-natural personality:
> Casual clothes with an athletic touch are for you.

The romantic personality:
> Your favorite styles are frilly and feminine.

The ingenue personality:
> The baby doll, girlish look is what you like best.

The contemporary personality:
> You prefer the fashionable look of toned-down fads.

12. **Don't forget the wardrobe basics.** These include things like jeans in denim and white, an ivory or white blouse, black or navy pants, and so on.

(Adapted from "How to Be a Smart Shopper,"
Brio magazine, October 1995)

eleven

An Overnight Sensation...Not!
Enjoying the Beauty Journey

*I*t was a Cinderella kind of thing. Meegan emerged from the long white limo with Trevor, her drop-dead gorgeous date. She stood at the top of the stairs taking in the beauty of the ballroom (and allowing her classmates the time to notice she had arrived!).

The sequins on her emerald green gown shimmered in the twinkling lights. Soft locks of hair framed her face just the way she had requested of her stylist. The way she shadowed her eyes had proved as intriguing as she had hoped. She looked more sophisticated tonight than usual. But this night was special. Senior prom.

Meegan and Trevor began to descend the stairs. Meegan smiled graciously at Crystal, class president and lifelong friend. Then she saw Kim and they exchanged an excited and warm glance.

Meegan slowly scanned the crowd, feeling grateful for all of her wonderful friends until her eyes locked with Suzanne's. Ha! Suzanne. The smile dropped from her lips, her eyes narrowed. *That sneaky little tramp, how dare she try to steal Trevor from me,* Meegan silently chided. *I showed her! I'm the one he's with tonight. She can eat her heart out. She can just—.*

W-w-w-hoa!

Smack!

Meegan was flat on her face! On the last step her right heel got tripped up in the hem of her gown and down she went! One minute elegant and in control, the next minute in a heap on the floor!

Gee, could that snide attitude toward Suzanne have stolen her focus and snagged her beauty—inside and out?

Yep!

And would you believe it? In Meegan's devotional book that very morning she'd read a lesson on forgiveness—you know, letting go of grudges! And there she was, harboring a big one against Suzanne!

As she slowly lifted herself from the cold marble tile, she lifted a quick apology to God.

"Sorry, Father. Will I ever have this inner beauty thing down pat? Will I ever be the kind, loving, forgiving person you want me to be?"

Meegan was learning a vital lesson!

I can relate! When I realized it was my heart the Lord most wanted to be beautiful, I started working on it! But it seemed that when I'd get one area shaped up, the Lord would shine his spotlight on yet another area and oh, boy, here we'd go again! The Holy Spirit and I would have to clean up and reconstruct another section of my heart!

God's Not Finished with You Yet!

This inner beauty stuff takes time!

We can't expect to be overnight sensations! We can't expect to suddenly ooze graciousness, always doing and saying the kindest thing in the kindest way.

It's a process!!

It's a journey!!

Not a journey to be feared, a journey to be enjoyed! And it *is* possible to take delight in the fact that you and the Lord are actively at work with the same goal in mind:

An unbelievably beautiful you!

Take heart in this heart-building business! You do not build alone. In fact, you build very little. The Lord does the heavy-duty work! And he won't quit until he's done! He promises in Philippians 1:6 (NIV),

> He who began a good work in you will carry it on to completion until the day of Christ Jesus.

That's great news. No need to get discouraged! God's not finished with you yet!

He is continually at work building the character of Christ and the inner beauty qualities of the Holy Spirit in you! That is what counts in the long run! We're talking about the part of you that will last into eternity—not your physical body!

God builds beauty that lasts and lasts! He gives you value and worth! He lavishes you with his love, allowing you to blossom into the beautiful woman he already sees you as! He fills you with his Spirit, who brings to you the beautiful qualities of love, joy, peace, patience, kindness, goodness, faithfulness, gentleness, and self-control!

And that's not all! He grants you specific gifts and talents that you get to use to serve him!

God makes us beautiful inside *and* out! He's the one who makes *real* beauty possible!

But wait! Can he do it completely alone? Is there something we can do to help? Any secrets to speeding up the beauty process just a pinch?

Yep!

You'll be on the beauty fast track when you offer God a heart that serves Christ and is surrendered to Christ! This is a heart in which God can grow inner beauty and reap a full, rich harvest!

Let's tune in to each of these time-saving secrets. There are a few beautiful Marys that I want you to meet. Each has a secret to share.

Secrets to the Inner-Beauty Fast Track!

The Servant Secret

She wasn't much older than you. Maybe younger! Her life was rolling along like anyone else's. She had recently gotten engaged to a fine man, a local carpenter.

She was quiet and humble, an ordinary girl who loved God. She was devout in her dedication to God and his Word.

She was Mary.

The one whose life changed dramatically when the angel Gabriel dropped in to inform her that God had chosen her to bear his son.

Can you imagine it? Mary could have freaked and refused! She had read of a coming Savior, but *her* as his mother? What would this do to her reputation? What would her fiancé Joseph think? How would she explain this one to her parents? Was she ready for kids—she could barely think past the honeymoon!

Yet, Mary's response was none of these. She had a servant's heart. She said to Gabriel, "I am the Lord's servant, and I am willing to do whatever he wants. May everything you said come true" (Luke 1:38, TLB).

The dictionary definition of *servant* is one that performs duties for a master. Mary was honored to be able to serve her master. She referred to herself as a "bondslave" (NAS), meaning a slave by choice! No one forced her to serve God, she chose to. Her servant heart was a fertile soil that God could use! And boy, did he! He used this ordinary girl in the most extraordinary way—to be the one who birthed his very own son!

You, too, can choose to have a servant's heart. God will do extraordinarily beautiful things in your life when you give it to him.

The Surrender Secret

To surrender simply means to give the control of your life over to the Lord, putting him in the driver's seat while you slide over and become the passenger! It simply means your desire to please God is greater than your desire to please yourself.

Wait. Did I say simply? Doesn't sound like a simple thing to do! Yet, it is a secret ingredient to having a life that radiates with beauty—a life that shines like a light in the darkness because it has been laid at the feet of Jesus.

A life like Mary's.

No, not Mary, mother of Jesus! Mary, the sister of Martha and Lazarus. The Mary who could always be found sitting at the feet of Jesus listening to his every word. The Mary who bowed before Jesus, anointing his feet with perfume and wiping them with her hair, all in preparation for his burial, for she knew from God's Word that the Savior would give his life. The Mary who fell at Jesus' feet after her brother, Lazarus, died, knowing that Jesus was still in control. Knowing that she had a God she could trust. She was probably the least surprised when Jesus raised Lazarus from the dead!

Mary's heart was surrendered to the Lord. She desired to please him, to worship him, to learn from him.

Mary is an excellent example for you and me. Her surrendered heart produced a sensitivity, an intimate knowing that made her spiritually aware. It produced a trust in God that was unshakable. Her sensitivity and trust served as a witness to others.

Mary is known even today for her surrendered heart, her beautiful heart. You can be known for that, too! Are you ready and willing to surrender all to Jesus?

The Sold Out Secret

She faithfully worked in the mills alongside her mother from a tender age. As a young teen she was the primary wage earner in the family. She endured an alcoholic father who, in a drunken state, kicked her out of the house.

But this young girl from Dundee, Scotland, named Mary Slessor knew she had a heavenly Father who loved her immensely. She knew from reading the Bible that he loved others, too, and she wanted to tell them! In her early twenties, Mary felt God call her to mission work in Calibar, West Africa. With great excitement, she left friends, family, and home and sailed to the jungles of Africa to share the love of Christ with a savage tribe who practiced witchcraft. She ventured into the area of Okoyong where no single women—and where no white person—had ever been.

Mary's courage and confidence came from Christ. She did not let her fear stop her from building the churches, schools, and medical outposts she knew were God's plan.

She did not allow anything to stand in the way of God's call. Telling people the story of Jesus and demonstrating his love for them was her life. It came first, no matter what the cost. Mary died at age sixty-six in a mud hut, deep in the heart of West Africa with the people she loved and had given her life to serve.

Incredible!

Mary was **sold out** to God! She stood firm, refusing to compromise God's call for her life. She was unwilling to settle for less than God's best.

Being sold out to the Lord means offering yourself 100 percent to him. It means offering him a heart that is completely his, one that won't turn back or compromise. A heart *he* can trust!

When you are sold out to the Lord, the beauty-building process is easier, quicker, and more effective! God knows you will respond positively as he molds and shapes your life as he desires. You are clay in the Potter's hands. How beautiful!

The Study Secret

Did you notice something that all three Marys had in common (other than their name, of course)? Each of them knew God's Word! Mary, Jesus' mother, knew that the Old Testament taught of a coming Savior. Mary, Martha's sister, knew that Jesus had to die for us, so she anointed him for burial. Mary Slessor knew Jesus' command to go into all the world preaching the gospel and making disciples of all men.

When you spend time in God's presence digging into his Word, you are tilling the soil of your heart, preparing it to serve, surrender, and sell out to God! This Word, growing in *your* heart, will cause you to shine with a beauty that comes from within!

Up Close and Personal
with *Contemporary Christian Artist* *Rebecca St. James*

Ask Rebecca where she turns for wisdom and encouragement, and she says the Bible! "It's so practical," she says, "and it's such a cool book. I try to read it as often as possible, and I keep daily devotions. It's sometimes hard with schedules, and it's so easy to come up with an excuse for not spending time in the Word. That's when we need to remember Ephesians 3:20: 'With God's power working in us, God can do much more than anything we can ask or imagine.' Isn't that wonderful?!

"The Bible shows us where our priorities should be and how to live a happy and joyful life. Our generation, especially, is bombarded with so much bad stuff—drugs, alcohol, teen pregnancy, abortion. It's all so sad. And yet God is still there, waiting to encourage and help us avoid those things—just look in the Bible!"

And to keep God's encouragement handy, Rebecca makes a habit of jotting down verses in a book or on notecards, then glancing at them throughout the day. "I really appreciate verses that challenge me. A favorite of mine is Proverbs 3:4-6, which says, 'If you want favor with both God and man, and a reputation for good judgment and common sense, then trust the Lord completely; don't ever trust yourself. In everything you do, put God first, and he will direct you and crown your efforts with success' (TLB)."

(Adapted from "Say G'Day To Rebecca St. James,"
Brio magazine, January 1995)

Rebecca is right! In a heart that serves, surrenders, sells out, and studies God's Word, the Lord can do "far more than we would ever dare to ask or even dream of—infinitely beyond our highest prayers, desires, thoughts, or hopes" (Ephesians 3:20, TLB).

God's Word in you will produce a bundle of beauty. You will catch yourself saying loving things, granting others grace and forgiveness, having more patience and peace, bubbling with a joy from deep within. You are on your way!

Be a servant! Be surrendered! Be sold out! Be a student of God's Word! These are the secret ingredients you can contribute to building a beautiful you!

Makeup won't do it. The finest skin care products won't do it! The latest hairstyle won't do it! The coolest clothes won't do it, either!

Now that you have read this entire book and have discovered what true beauty is and how it becomes yours, let's find out how you're doing in applying these truths.

THE BEAUTIFUL YOU CHECKLIST

1. Do you believe that in God's eyes you have a beauty that is yours alone and that you truly are positively *awesome*?
   ☐ Yep! ☐ Nope! ☐ Working on It!

2. Are you thankful for each of the unique details in your appearance that make you one-of-a-kind, a true work of art?
   ☐ Yep! ☐ Nope! ☐ Working on It!

3. Have you developed patience with your look, knowing that as you grow and change, your look will do the same?
   ☐ Yep! ☐ Nope! ☐ Working on It!

4. Is forgiving others when they tease you a little easier now?
   ☐ Yep! ☐ Nope! ☐ Working on It!

5. Are you celebrating your looks instead of comparing them to others?
   ☐ Yep! ☐ Nope! ☐ Working on It!

6. Are you convinced that beauty is a whole lot more than physical attractiveness?
   ☐ Yep! ☐ Nope! ☐ Working on It!

7. Can you look at ads and magazine covers with a critical eye, knowing that much of what you see is not real?
   ☐ Yep! ☐ Nope! ☐ Working on It!

8. Are you glad you're *not* a Barbie, but a real girl with a real heart?
   ☐ Yep! ☐ Nope! ☐ Working on It!

9. Are you letting go of the dream to look like a cover girl?
   ☐ Yep!   ☐ Nope!   ☐ Working on It!

10. Are you using the light, natural, color-coordinated makeup techniques that enhance your natural beauty?
    ☐ Yep!   ☐ Nope!   ☐ Working on It!

11. Are you feeding your body the fuel it needs to look and feel its best?
    ☐ Yep!   ☐ Nope!   ☐ Working on It!

12. Are you eating lots of fresh fruits and veggies and drinking six to eight glasses of water per day?
    ☐ Yep!   ☐ Nope!   ☐ Working on It!

13. How's your "temple"? Clean, fit, and healthy?
    ☐ Yep!   ☐ Nope!   ☐ Working on It!

14. Are you respecting yourself with good grooming and an active and drug-free lifestyle?
    ☐ Yep!   ☐ Nope!   ☐ Working on It!

15. Have you made a commitment to abstinence?
    ☐ Yep!   ☐ Nope!   ☐ Working on It!

16. Are you basking in God's unconditional, unselfish, forgiving, and unending love?
    ☐ Yep!   ☐ Nope!   ☐ Working on It!

17. Are you free to be yourself, knowing that the One who knows you best, loves you most?
    ☐ Yep!   ☐ Nope!   ☐ Working on It!

18. Are you excited that your adequacy, confidence, and value come from Christ (*not* from your appearance)?
    ☐ Yep!   ☐ Nope!   ☐ Working on It!

19. Are you working on developing a Christ-like heart, full of the fruit of the Holy Spirit?
    ☐ Yep!   ☐ Nope!   ☐ Working on It!

20. Have you found ways to put your God-given gifts and talents to use for the Lord?
    ☐ Yep!   ☐ Nope!   ☐ Working on It!

21. Are you investing your efforts on your inner beauty knowing that it lasts into eternity?
    ☐ Yep!   ☐ Nope!   ☐ Working on It!

22. Is your spirit becoming more gentle, granting grace and mercy to others?
    ☐ Yep!   ☐ Nope!   ☐ Working on It!

23. And quiet? Are you prayed-up, trusting God in all things?
    ☐ Yep!   ☐ Nope!   ☐ Working on It!

24. Are you getting closer to being a Proverbs 31 gal?
    ☐ Yep!   ☐ Nope!   ☐ Working on It!

25. Are you known for being kind and good?
    ☐ Yep!   ☐ Nope!   ☐ Working on It!

26. Are you giving yourself wholeheartedly to God, trusting that he is working with you to build a beautiful you?
    ☐ Yep!   ☐ Nope!   ☐ Working on It!

27. Are you ready to surrender to the Lord, have a servant attitude and be sold out to him?

    ☐ Yep!   ☐ Nope!   ☐ Working on It!

28. Will you commit to studying God's Word on a consistent basis?

    ☐ Yep!   ☐ Nope!   ☐ Working on It!

I just know that you are well on your way to being the best *you* possible!

You are entering the prime of your existence! You have your whole life ahead of you. You can start now to move forward with great confidence! You are beautiful on the outside, just as the Master Designer planned, *and* you are on the inner beauty journey, working with the Holy Spirit to build a beautiful you on the inside!

Now is the time to begin building beautiful relationships, fond memories, and a reputation that brings warm thoughts of you to others and glory to the Father!

Up Close and Personal
with Contemporary Christian Singer
Pam Thum

We all want to look good, but Pam now knows it's what's *inside* that counts. "None of us knows how much time we have to live," Pam says. "What do we want people to say when we're gone? 'My, she was a pretty girl'? Hopefully, our goals go much deeper than that."

When thinking of how she wants to be remembered Pam reflects on a special relative. "My Aunt Myrtle died three years ago," she says. "She looked like Aunt Bea from the 'Andy Griffith Show.' Her eyes twinkled all the time. She was forever wiping perspiration from her brow because she was like a little tornado.

"She was short and sweet—very plump. When she hugged me, I felt like GOD was hugging me. She baked cookies and taught Sunday school. My friends met her and wanted to hang out with her when I left town.

"I sang at her funeral, and the place was packed around July 4 when most people are out of town. Wealthy people with jewels dripping off them walked by me and said, 'Your aunt changed our lives because of her love for God and people.'

"Little children and teens came by just sobbing, saying how much they were going to miss her. One lady told me it had been eight months since she'd taken a drink. 'I'm an alcoholic,' she said. 'And nobody believed in me anymore except your Aunt Myrtle. She used to pray for me and come by and pick me up at the street corner and bring me to church. Now it's been eight months since I've had a drink.'

"THAT'S how I want to be remembered. Like my Aunt Myrtle—someone who loved God with all her heart and loved people as she loved herself. Those people gave up their holiday and came to her funeral. Not because she was skinny and pretty. And it wasn't because of clothes, riches, or a fancy car. She had none of those things. It was because of *her* obedience to Christ that *their* lives were changed.

> "That puts it all in perspective, doesn't it? When we get our eyes on Jesus, we focus on others, and we won't have the obsessive need to be perfect."
>
> (Taken from "Pam Thum: Free To Be Herself!"
> *Brio* magazine, July 1994)

Wise words from a wonderful lady. Gives us all something to contemplate! Have you ever thought about how you'd like to be remembered? Take a sec to prayerfully consider all we've chatted about in this book.

Really do it. Pause!

Your Letter to the Lord

Now, write a letter to the Lord, sharing with him how you want to be remembered.

$Date$ _____

Dear Lord,

_____

_____

_____

_____

_____

_____

_____

_____

_____

_____

_____

_____

_____

_____

_____

_____

_____

_____

_____

Yours forever,

Reread what you just wrote.

Use this letter as a guideline to live your life every day. Start now!

You are well on your way to becoming a truly beautiful woman.

Yep.

You are positively awesome!

SEMINARS AND RETREATS AVAILABLE
with *Andrea Stephens*

I'm Glad You Know Where We're Going, Lord!
Discovering God's direction in your life.

God Thinks You're Positively Awesome!
Teaching girls to love their looks!

You Want Me to W-W-W-W-Witness?
Learn how easy it is to tell others about Christ every day!

Being God's Kids in a Tough Teen World
Uncover the secret of putting God first
in four important areas of your life!

Stressed Out, but Hangin' Tough!
Find out God's answer for handling stress,
plus tons of practical tips!

The Importance of Being You!
Learn how to boost your self-esteem and appreciate your
unique personality, gifts, and talents!

Glamour to Glory
From Model to Minister's Wife!
Andrea Stephens' personal testimony.

FOR MORE INFORMATION CONTACT:
ANDREA STEPHENS
P.O. BOX 2856
BAKERSFIELD, CA 93303

Check out these other great books for teens!

Anybody Got a Clue About Guys?

A Young Woman's Guide to Healthy Relationships
SUSIE SHELLENBERGER

Susie Shellenberger, editor of Focus on the Family's *Brio* magazine, offers "big sister" insights into understanding and relating to the opposite sex. **$10.99** ISBN 0-89283-911-2

If the Pasta Wiggles, Don't Eat It!

Wise Words to Tickle Your Funny Bone and Make You Think
MARTHA BOLTON

Includes ninety fun devotions to start your day. Martha Bolton is the "Cafeteria Lady" of *Brio* magazine. **$10.99** ISBN 0-89283-852-3

Life Is Like Driver's Ed...

Ya Gotta Buckle Up, Stay to the Right, and Watch those Turns!
Devotions for Teens and Their Parents
GREG JOHNSON

Whether you read these alone or discuss them with your parents these devotions—based on the Book of Psalms—are a great way to help you stay "on track" with God. **$10.99**
ISBN 0-89283-961-9